The Boy on the Bicycle:

A Forgotten Case of Wrongful Conviction in Toronto

BY NATE HENDLEY

FIVE RIVERS PUBLISHING

WWW.FIVERIVERSPUBLISHING.COM

Five Rivers Publishing, 704 Queen Street, P.O. Box 293, Neustadt, ON N0G 2M0, Canada.

www.fiveriverspublishing.com

The Boy on the Bicycle, Copyright © 2018 by Nate Hendley.

Edited by Lorina Stephens

Cover Copyright © 2018 by Jeff Minkevics.

Interior design and layout by Éric Desmarais.

Titles set in Erika Ormig by Peter Wiegel. Designed to look like a typewriter font with uneven ink spread and used for display and titles.

Text set in EB Garamond by Georg Duffner. It intended to be an excellent, classical, Garamond. It is a community project to create a revival of Claude Garamont's famous humanist typefaces from the mid-16th century.

Published in Canada

Library and Archives Canada Cataloguing in Publication

Hendley, Nate, author

The boy on the bicycle : a forgotten case of wrongful conviction in Toronto / by Nate Hendley.

Issued in print and electronic formats.

ISBN 978-1-988274-51-5 (softcover).

ISBN 978-1-988274-52-2 (EPUB)

1. Moffatt, Ron. 2. Murder Ontario Toronto. 3. Trials (Murder) Ontario-- Toronto. 4. Judicial error Ontario Toronto. I. Title.

HV6535.C33T67 2018 364.152'309713541 C2018-900865-2

C2018-900866-0

THIS BOOK IS DEDICATED TO RONALD MOFFATT AND HIS FAMILY, PAST AND PRESENT.

Contents

Foreword

The murder of seven-year-old Wayne Mallette on the grounds of the Canadian National Exhibition (CNE) in Toronto on Saturday, September 15, 1956, was a huge news story in its day. A story that has been largely forgotten, except perhaps when mentioned in connection with his actual murderer, serial killer Peter Woodcock.

The subsequent arrest, trial and conviction of 14-year-old Ron Moffatt—prime suspect in the case—was also huge news. So was Moffatt's retrial—and the dawning realization that he had been convicted of a crime he didn't commit.

Toronto had three big newspapers at the time— *The Globe and Mail,* the *Toronto Daily Star* and *The Telegram.* All of these papers wrote extensively about the case. Because he was tried as a juvenile, not an adult, Moffatt's name was never mentioned in this coverage.

In the 1950s, the legislation governing young offenders (that is, suspects under 18) was the Juvenile Delinquents Act. The current legislation regarding underage suspects is the Youth Criminal Justice Act. Like the Juvenile Delinquents Act, the Youth Criminal

Justice Act is national in scope (all criminal law is federal in Canada) and forbids the media from publicizing the names of young offenders. There are exceptions to this rule, however.

"Information identifying a young person's involvement in the criminal justice system can be published [in some circumstances] ... Where a young person has turned 18, he or she may publish or agree to the publication of their information provided they are not in custody at the time of publication," reads an online notice at the Department of Justice website, regarding current legislation.

Needless to say, Ron Moffatt meets this standard and is very eager to have his full name used and his story told.

Telling that story proved more difficult than I anticipated, however.

While there's no shortage of archival newspaper material on Moffatt's case, official documents proved much harder to come by. I made a Freedom of Information request with the Toronto Police Service for memos, reports and other documents relating to the case, and received nothing (despite frequent phone calls on my part, to the person looking into my request).

Trial and court-related documents were also difficult to track down. Material from older Toronto trials are stored with the Archives of Ontario. When I contacted the Archives, I was told they required administrative information (including the transfer number, file number, schedule number and temporary box number) of any relevant court files before they could hunt for such documents. I went to several courthouses in person, made phone calls and emails and wrote letters, but no one seemed to have the administrative information I needed. I was informed several times by court clerks that they couldn't possibly locate such data. A private company that specialized in tracking down Ontario court transcripts couldn't help either. They only dealt with recent trials. The 1950s was ancient history for them.

I tried another approach. I made Freedom of Information requests for specific documents with the Ontario Ministry of Government and Consumer Services. If not court transcripts, then perhaps other files that might be useful for my research. I included the specific title of domestic case files in the York Judicial District Provincial Court system (which included Toronto) from 1956 and 1957. I also requested York Crown Attorney prosecution files for the same years. In all cases the results were the same: nada. No documents relating to Moffatt's two trials were found. A request to the Ministry of the Attorney General of Ontario was equally fruitless. I also contacted the Canadian National Exhibition (CNE) Archives and was told they had no records of the Wayne Mallette murder on file.

In terms of the court material, it's highly probable most of these documents have been destroyed. There's nothing sinister about this practice. Not everything makes it to the Archives of Ontario. Until recently, documents from a court trial would be stored in boxes or saved on either microfiche or microfilm. The problem is, even an average criminal trial, on a non-violent charge, can generate an enormous amount of paperwork. Storing paper copies of all these documents would require a huge amount of space. Putting all these documents on microfiche or microfilm would be enormously expensive. So, in the past, many court documents were simply destroyed after a period of time, usually a few decades. For anyone interested, the website of the Court Services Division of the Ministry of the Ontario Attorney General contains information about document retention practices from the past. Today, digitization makes it far easier to retain all kinds of documents for future reference.

I'm not the first researcher to be faced with this problem. When investigators sought to re-examine the 1959 murder conviction of Steven Truscott in the late 1990s, it was discovered that all physical evidence from the case held by the Center for Forensic Sciences had been discarded years before. Again, there is nothing conspiratorial about this, it is simply a matter of making space for new evidence from more recent cases.

Fortunately, I received a treasure trove of police documents about the Moffatt case from a fellow crime writer. These photocopied documents from the 1950s included police memos, teletype messages, letters, wanted posters, autopsy reports and judicial verdicts. The most vital document was a copy of Ron Moffatt's "confession" to police. This confession (made under extreme duress) is what convicted Moffatt at his first trial. There was very little other evidence against him, except speculation. These documents provided vital information about the Moffatt case that wasn't forthcoming from official channels.

This was not the only source of original material I used for my book, however. Staff at the Law Society of Upper Canada Archives at Osgoode Hall in Toronto were extremely helpful and allowed me into their offices to view rare material. The LSUC Archives contain a large number of files donated by defence attorney Goldwin Arthur Martin and his star lawyer, Patrick Hartt. Hartt was the lawyer who won an appeal to grant Moffatt a second trial, then fought courageously to free the teenager when it became apparent someone else had killed Wayne Mallette. The LSUC Archives contain letters, speeches and other documents relating to the case. One of the more poignant items I examined was a day planner from Martin's law firm, with the name *Moffatt* (misspelled as *Moffat*) written in pencil on dates from 1957. The Law Society of Upper Canada (LSUC) is now called the Law Society of Ontario. It was known as the Law Society of Upper Canada, however, when I visited the Archives and that is how I referred to the regulatory body throughout this manuscript.

My girlfriend Jeanne Enright, world's finest partner and a librarian at the Toronto Reference Library, also helped me track down several important but obscure sources of information. These included a lengthy report to Toronto's Board of Commissioners of Police detailing crime in 1956 (the report mentioned Moffatt by name) and documents relating to the Ontario Training School for Boys in Bowmanville, Ontario and the Ontario Reformatory, Guelph.

In addition to providing valuable information that was used in this book, crime author Mark Bourrie offered chilling insights into the mind and methods of serial killer Peter Woodcock. As Woodcock was dead by the time I started this project, I drew on previously published accounts of his actions to round out my characterization of the man. I recommend Bourrie's 1997 book, *By Reason of Insanity* and subsequent revised e-book, *Peter Woodcock: Canada's Youngest Serial Killer*, for anyone interested in getting a sense of Woodcock's depraved nature.

Of course, my single most helpful resource was Ron Moffatt himself. Over the years, I interviewed Moffatt via phone, email, Skype and in-person. He always responded with dignity and a wealth of detail. While Moffatt's case has been mentioned in a few recent books and newspaper articles (which, like this book, cite Moffatt by name), this is the first full-length account of the horrors he went through in the 1950s.

It was important that Moffatt was so informative. Given how long ago his case took place, almost all the major players involved, save Moffatt, are dead. Fortunately, the voices and personalities of many of these people have been preserved, in the form of letters, memos, court rulings and comments to the press.

Ideally, I would like to see Moffatt receive compensation for his wrongful conviction and time served. Although he was in custody less than a year, the experience marked him for life. It is to Moffatt's credit that he pulled himself together and enjoyed a successful career and family-life. At the very least, authorities owe Moffatt an apology for his terrible treatment.

As I discovered, false confessions to police are unfortunately common. I offer details in this book as to why suspects confess to crimes they didn't commit.

It is my hope that modern DNA testing will lower the rate of wrongful convictions so fewer people have to endure what Ronald Moffatt suffered.

Introduction - Wayne

Saturday, September 15, 1956

Seven year-old Wayne Richard Mallette idled on the veranda of his grandmother's house at 42 Empress Crescent, in Toronto's west-end. It was dusk, and Wayne and his family had just finished supper. The youngest in a family of boys, Wayne was set to start grade two within a few days. Earlier that day, the fair-haired, brown-eyed child had travelled with his parents and brothers from Seeley's Bay, a small community near Kingston, Ontario, where the Mallette family lived.

Built up along Lake Ontario, Toronto was only a fraction of its current size, but for small-town visitors like the Mallette family, it was a major metropolis. The 1956 Census recorded 667,706 people in Toronto, making it the second-biggest city in Canada, after Montreal.

Wayne's father, John, was 49 years-old and worked as a machine operator for an aluminum company in Kingston. His mother, Irene, was 43. It was Irene's mother—Mrs. Hazel Armstrong—whom the family was visiting. Mrs. Armstrong lived in south Parkdale, a community located near the grounds of the Canadian

National Exhibition (CNE). 'The Ex' was an annual event held from late August to early September that featured amusement park rides, carnival games, entertainers and agricultural displays. The CNE had closed for the season, and the vast Exhibition grounds were empty.

Three of Wayne's brothers—John, who was 21, Graham who was 17, and Ronald, who was 11—were rambling around the house. A fifth brother named Dale, who was nine, remained at home in Seeley's Bay. The family had no daughters.

Around 7 p.m., John and Graham announced they wanted to go to the movies. Wayne asked his older brothers to take him with them, but they didn't want their younger sibling tagging along. John and Graham left their grandmother's house and Wayne wandered onto the front lawn to play. Wayne eventually strolled from the front yard in the direction of the CNE. His likely mission was to visit a nearby Canadian National Railway line that passed through the area. Like many young boys, Wayne was fascinated by trains.

Wayne's family observed him wandering off: "Wayne Mallette was last seen at about 7:15 p.m. by his brother, Ronald, when entering the Canadian National Exhibition Grounds," noted a subsequent police report.

Wayne meandered and was soon out of sight of his family. The child encountered another young person out enjoying the night air. It was a boy on a bicycle, a teenager with black hair, a pimply face and horn-rimmed glasses. The teenager wore a grey windbreaker, dark pants and a white T-shirt with red stripes. He wasn't particularly tall or impressive looking, but he had a top-of-the-line, red-coloured bicycle and seemed friendly. Wayne had no way of knowing his new acquaintance was a highly disturbed 17-year-old with a history of behavioural problems and a pattern of molesting children.

At some point, the dark-haired teen suggested Wayne come with him to a place west of the Dufferin Gate on the CNE grounds. It was a great spot to watch trains, said the stranger. The little boy went off obligingly with this new pal.

From what was later recollected in court statements and police documents, the dark-haired teen tried to engage in some kind of sex game with Wayne. The teenager had done the same thing with plenty of other kids, during regular bicycle prowls around the city. Only Wayne didn't want to play and grew scared. The teen turned from friendly to furious. He pushed the little boy's face into the dirt. He assaulted the child with his feet and hands, even biting him on the legs. The attacker watched Wayne die then left on his bike.

Around the same time, night watchman George Sinclair was beginning his rounds at the CNE. He was patrolling near the Pure Food Building when he was approached by a chatty youth on a bicycle. The boy asked if Sinclair was a police officer. When told no, the teenager's inquiries grew stranger. The boy asked Sinclair if he "ever found any bodies" in the bushes on the Exhibition grounds. Sinclair offered a non-committal response. The youth asked what he would do if he did find a body? The kid also mentioned he had seen a suspicious looking teen running away from the area "who is a perfect double for me."

Naturally, Sinclair found all of this deeply unsettling. He tried to change the subject several times "but the youth kept returning the conversation to the murders," noted a police memo.

The boy mentioned he was interested in flying, that he might belong to the Air Cadets (Sinclair wasn't sure of his exact comment). The kid said he lived "North of Toronto" then took off on his bicycle, riding north on Strachan Avenue.

Sinclair had an eye for detail and later gave police a good description of the weird kid he had encountered: "14 – 16 years, slight build, over 5', hair thought to be dark, seemed to be parted and combed to one side; hair straight but not a crew cut; thin face, seemed to stay behind watchman but believed to be wearing dark cloth windbreaker, dark pants, spoke quickly, well-spoken in boyish voice, bicycle seemed to be full size, thought not to be a racer, dark colour," read a police memo.

Irene Mallette of course knew nothing of this strange encounter. Back at her mother's house, she fretted over her missing son. John Mallette assured her that Wayne had probably joined his older brothers at the movies. Irene wasn't convinced. The first call to police from the house was made at 8:15 p.m. Wayne's mother sat by a window, waiting anxiously for her older sons to return, hopefully with Wayne in tow.

At around 10 p.m., John and Graham returned to Empress Crescent. Wayne was not with them. A second, more urgent call was made to police. Constables soon arrived from the Cowan Avenue station. Police began searching the area for the missing boy. Wayne's father joined the search. A group of about 30 policemen began poking around trees and bushes on the CNE grounds. It was a moonless night, so the police used flashlights to make their search.

A teletype message was sent to city police stations about the missing boy, along with a description. Mallette was described as "7 years. Male, white, slender build, fair complexion, blond hair, brown eyes, scar on left wrist, neatly dressed, wearing a blue blazer, blue nylon shirt, brown shoes."

A search was launched by officers from the No. 6 division, later joined by police from No. 1 division. Toronto Harbour Police were alerted, to check the waterfront near the Exhibition grounds, to see if the little boy had fallen into Lake Ontario. The teletype message about Mallette was repeated at 2:15 a.m.

Then, a tragic follow-up message: "Boy Located."

He was found by Constables Jack Smith and Robert Brown, at roughly the same time the second teletype went out. While searching the fairgrounds, the policemen shined their flashlights on a secluded clump of bushes and small trees, roughly 100 yards west of the Dufferin Gate. Near a chain-link fence that separated the Exhibition grounds from railroad tracks, the two men found the lifeless body of a child. It was a boy, lying on his back. His clothing hadn't been disturbed and there were "no apparent injuries to the body" though there were "dirt marks on side of face and scratch marks on right side of neck," stated a police report.

Authorities brought John Mallette to the scene, who confirmed the body was that of his son. The devastated father returned to Empress Crescent, in the company of a police officer, to report the grim findings to his wife. Irene Mallette promptly collapsed. A doctor was brought in who sedated the distraught mother. Police called Coroner Doctor Morton Shulman to the crime scene. Dr. Shulman confirmed what was already very apparent—that the little boy was dead. Then, he ordered the body taken to the Coroner's office.

Police began searching the area for clues immediately after Mallette's remains were removed. The crime scene was guarded by uniformed policemen.

Police took John Mallette to the morgue, to make a formal identification of his son. The formal ID was made at 4:45 a.m. An autopsy was begun roughly three hours later. One of the policemen present at the post-mortem examination was Sergeant of Detectives Bernard Simmonds. A well-respected officer, Simmonds had also been at the Mallette crime scene. Det. Simmonds helped mark evidence, including Mallette's clothing, then passed these crime scene exhibits to the Ontario Attorney General's Laboratory. The autopsy noted the presence of bite marks on one of Mallette's legs.

Police continued to search the Exhibition grounds. Samples were taken of the soil and even from trees in the area, in the hope they might turn up some forensic evidence.

In a city with a low crime rate, in a more innocent era where sex crimes were only whispered about, Wayne's death was shocking news. The *Toronto Daily Star* ran a front page story about the slaying on September 17, 1956.

"There is no question it is a case of murder," Dr. Shulman told reporters.

"Coroner's department officials revealed the boy's body bore evidence of a vicious attack during which he was bitten. Death was caused by asphyxiation by pressing his face into the dirt while gripping him by the neck, police said," wrote the *Star*. Subsequent articles mentioned the night watchman's encounter with the dark-haired boy on a bicycle, who was now the prime suspect in the case.

Irene Mallette unleashed her rage and anguish to the press.

"But I never liked Toronto. It is a sinful city. Mothers here just don't know the things that can happen to their children. They have no idea. Happy cheerful little Wayne didn't know. He had been told about strangers. But what does that really mean to a seven-year-old? ... Somebody killed Wayne. Somebody killed him and carried him off ... I hate this city. But my husband, my sons and I are staying here until we get the persons who did this to Wayne. We're not leaving until we get him ... I pray God will forgive him. We can't," wrote the *Star*.

At the very same time Wayne was exploring the rail-line and the CNE fairgrounds, a teenage boy was enjoying a double-bill at the Metro Theatre at 677 Bloor Street West. Originally opened in the late 1930s, the Metro primarily featured second-run movies and 'B' films. Appropriately enough, on the night of September 15, 1956, a film made two years earlier called *Ulysses*, featuring Kirk Douglas was playing. The other film was an MGM western called *The Last Hunt*, with Robert Taylor. The movies, plus a cartoon, played between 5:30 – 9:15 p.m. that evening (an earlier screening had taken place that afternoon).

In later decades, the Metro would become notorious for showing adult movies. At the time, it was merely a convenient spot for 14-year-old Ron Moffatt to take in some flicks with friends. One of his pals was employed as an usher at the Metro. Ron sat with his friend's girlfriend, and enjoyed the double-bill.

Moffatt's life was somewhat dysfunctional. His father, Omar Moffatt, worked as a punch-press operator. Both Omar and his wife, Bette Moffatt, enjoyed boisterous nights of heavy drinking, which could lead to quarrels and other disruptions. Ron and his two younger brothers did the best they could to manage.

Ron Moffatt was no angel himself. When younger, he had a brush with the law for committing a break and enter at St. Lawrence Market with a teenage boy. For the summer of 1956, however, he had been gainfully employed at the CNE, offering demonstrations of a ride called 'The Rotor'. People would enter this ride, which then spun around at high-speed. The floor would drop out but the CNE patrons would be safely stuck to the wall, as the ride continued to spin.

It had been a bustling season at the CNE that year. Two main attractions included 'singing cowboy' Gene Autry and Annie Oakley (not the actual female sharpshooter of the same name, but an actress named Gail Davis who played the western femme fatale on a TV show). A photograph of Davis, complete with cowboy hat and pistol made the front page of the *Toronto Daily Star* on August 30, 1956. The accompanying article noted Davis' presence during an advance tour of the CNE by some "1,100 underprivileged children."

Newspaper advertisements heralded various commercial exhibits at the CNE, including 'The Plainsman'—a rather boxy looking station wagon—and a display of pianos and organs from a music store. In a reflection of the times, the September 1 edition of the *Daily Star* grimly informed readers of a "secret visit" made by "12 unidentified Russians" to the CNE. As it turned out, the Russians were from the Soviet Fisheries Ministry, on an official tour of Canadian fishing sites and simply wanted to see the Ex. The initial front-page headlines, however, exemplified the Cold War paranoia of the day.

Back at the Metro, Ron Moffatt watched the two movies then spent some time assisting the theatre owner change the lettering on the theatre sign. Instead of returning to his family residence at 39 Vanauley Street,

Apartment 2, in downtown Toronto, Moffatt stayed over at a friend's house. He remained oblivious to the search going on for the killer of Wayne Mallette.

In a little over a week's time, Ron Moffatt would find himself accused of murdering the little boy. Coerced into a false confession, he says, that led to a trial, months of detention and a lifetime of stress, fear and anger—a wrongful conviction for which Ron Moffatt never received a formal apology, much less compensation.

Moffatt's arrest would be spearheaded by a policeman known as "Canada's greatest detective" in some circles. A detective held in high esteem for his role in tracking down flamboyant bandit Edwin Alonzo Boyd, leader of the bank-robbing Boyd Gang in 1952.

The real killer, a misfit named Peter Woodcock, remained free to prowl Toronto streets on his bicycle. The dark-haired teenager with a bad complexion and thick glasses would continue molesting and killing children for months as Ron Moffatt languished in detention.

Chapter One - The Investigation

In the days following the discovery of Wayne Mallette's body, police tried to fit together the bits of evidence they had collected in the case. More than anything, police were almost certain the suspect was an adolescent boy, probably in his teens. This assumption was based on a couple of key facts. First, there was that strange encounter on the evening of the murder between a dark-haired teenaged boy with a bicycle and a night watchman at the CNE fairgrounds. Then, medical evidence came in that also pointed to a youthful suspect.

A piece published September 19, 1956 in the *Globe and Mail* referred to scratch marks found on Mallette's throat and bite marks on his calf

"The faint marks on the throat are too small to have been made by an adult's hand. The tooth marks on the leg is of a size to suggest a child or youth," noted the article.

Other medical evidence was also weighed. Blood and stomach content samples were sent to the Ontario Attorney-General's Laboratory, located at Queen's Park for testing. The conclusion was that the little boy had not been poisoned or drugged in any way before he died.

Police fanned out across the city, interviewing potential suspects and family members, visiting schools, following up on leads and talking to possible witnesses. Calls offering tips poured in to police investigators, most of them useless. Many callers reported recent sightings of sketchy looking men on the CNE grounds. Some of these men were tracked down, interviewed by police, and cleared. A few of the calls came from parents who claimed their boys had also been abused or molested by strangers at the CNE. None of these leads panned out.

Authorities also tried to convince the mysterious cyclist to speak with them.

"Inspector Adolphus Payne last night appealed to a youth seen riding his bicycle down the backroad through the CNE from the Pure Food Building to Strachan Ave. to come forward. The inspector said police believe the youth, about 15, five feet six inches in height and weighing 115 pounds, may be able to give some details of how [Wayne Mallette] died .... Banking strongly on the time angle—the bicyclist was seen at almost the exact time the boy is believed to have died—police feel the youth will be able to give them a detailed description of what took place. Insp. Payne said the cyclist was wearing a dark windbreaker and dark hat and riding a dark blue or black bicycle," stated the *Globe* on September 17.

The time angle referred to the youth's strange encounter with the night watchman at the CNE. Initial media reports said the encounter occurred around 9 p.m.

Inspector Payne's presence in the investigation was significant. Later described as "Canada's greatest detective", Payne was already a legend on the Toronto police force. Born in 1909, Payne became a cop two decades later and quickly earned a reputation as a determined officer with a systematic approach to law enforcement.

The inspector became a superstar in 1952 after tracking down master criminal Edwin Alonzo Boyd. Boyd headed a gang of bank robbers who staged a number of daring hold-ups in Toronto in the early 1950s. While the so-called Boyd Gang became media celebrities, they were actually a group of hardened criminals. Two members of the gang—Lennie Jackson and Steve Suchan—murdered a police officer named Detective Edmund Tong. Jackson and Suchan were hanged for this crime at the Don Jail.

Through a careful investigation and a clever sting operation, Payne determined that Boyd and his wife were holed up at 42 Heath Street in Toronto. Det. Payne and 50 armed cops conducted a night-time raid and caught Boyd and his wife while they were still asleep. The head of the Boyd Gang surrendered without resistance—good thing too, as there were five loaded handguns within his reach (plus a knife, ammunition and $23,329 in stolen bank money).

The raid, along with a photograph of Inspector Payne made the front-page story of the *Toronto Daily Star* on

March 17, 1952. The headline read, "Psychology, Logic, Brains, Alertness, Finally Courage Resulted in Boyd's Capture."

"It wasn't a tipster and it wasn't luck. It was a red-haired man with a ready grin, a friendly manner and half a lifetime of police experience. This man, and his intuition, brought a gun muzzle to Edwin Boyd's head at dawn on Saturday ... As Boyd stared, dazed, into a flashlight's beam, his first thought was "betrayal". And, in a way, he was right. His much-vaunted mind had done him dirt. He had under-rated police in general and one policeman in particular. This was the pay-off on brains and all he could do was blink," wrote the *Star*.

The article noted that Det. Payne was nicknamed "Trigger". His police peers gave him this moniker after an incident in which he forced the driver of a stolen car off the road by firing a single warning shot.

"Today, he is puttering about his beautiful North Toronto home. Tomorrow he'll be back on his usual job, checking stolen car lists. And he will, as always, do this job willingly and do it well—until another big task calls for his time and his talents," continued the *Star*.

Now, four years later, Inspector Payne was helping with another big task, and calling for the mystery cyclist to turn himself in. Police considered the dark-haired teen a potential witness—not a suspect—in Mallette's death, or so they claimed.

"The boy on the bicycle ... may be able to give

investigators some details on the youth who attacked Wayne," noted the *Star* on September 18.

Based on stomach content analysis, medical authorities estimated that Mallette died around 9 p.m. Future murder cases in Ontario would highlight the difficulty of estimating time of death based on stomach content. Still, the doctors' estimate coincided with the encounter between the night watchman and the fleeing cyclist. If the times were correct, the suspect must have crossed paths with the security guard almost immediately after Mallette died.

Beyond this, confusion still reigned in the case. While some officials, including city coroner, Dr. Morton Shulman, believed Wayne had been murdered, others weren't so certain. There was speculation by medical officers that Wayne might have died by accident as the result of "rough play" with an older boy.

Authorities were also uncertain if Mallette had been molested. In this more naïve era, it was difficult for people to even consider that little children could be the victims of sexual predators.

On Monday, September 17, the *Toronto Telegram* ran a front-page headline reading, "Pervert Suspected but Lad's Killing May be Mishap." One day later, a *Globe* headline authoritatively asserted, "Find Dead Boy at CNE Not Victim of Pervert." The *Star*, for its part, said that Mallette had been "choked to death by a sex pervert" in its coverage on September 17. "Police said Wayne may have been the victim of a sex deviate who has been chased out of High Park in [a] recent drive ...

last week five arrests were made in five days on indecency charges in the park," added the *Star*.

The report by Dr. Ward Smith, Director of the Ontario Attorney-General's Laboratory, said there was no evidence Mallette had been "indecently assaulted" as the *Globe* story delicately noted. The article spared readers any explanation as to how the doctor came to this conclusion. A later report from the Attorney-General's Laboratory would partly explain Dr. Smith's conclusion. According to this document, "no evidence of semen [was] found on any of the clothing" of Wayne Mallette—a fact the media considered too raw to comment on at the time.

For all that, authorities did investigate men's washrooms on the CNE grounds. Police also contacted "known frequenters" of said washrooms, as a September 17 police memo put it. It is unclear if police were simply being thorough or were considering the possibility that gay men who trolled such places were involved in Mallette's murder. The memo went into great detail about the location of the washrooms in question, but otherwise didn't offer any useful information about the case.

Police sent a circular to public and separate high schools across Toronto, asking for the boy on the bicycle to come forward. No one did. Authorities also took more proactive steps, interviewing a range of boys. A memo to Inspector John Nimmo dated September 18 listed half-a-dozen youths who had been investigated. The boys ranged in age from 11 to 14. Most had been seen at the Exhibition grounds on September 15. The list did not include the names of Ron Moffatt or Peter Woodcock.

According to the *Telegram*, a young man contacted police within hours of Mallette's murder, to confess to the crime. Two detectives—Frank Carter and Ralph Gilbert—met the suspect at his Queen Street West. home and took him in for questioning. They spoke with the 20-year-old for hours, concluding he had nothing to do with the death of Wayne Mallette. The young man was either disturbed or playing some kind of sick joke. Police charged him with public mischief and he was dropped from the list of serious suspects.

While Mallette's murder dominated Toronto headlines for days, it also had repercussions in smaller communities. The *Kingston-Whig Standard*—largest newspaper near the Mallette family's tiny hometown—ran the story for days on its front page. "Seeley's Bay Lad, 7, Said Murder Victim" read a banner headline, September 17. A reminder that this was as much a local tragedy as a major Toronto crime story. Toronto papers also ran photos of the grieving Mallette family and multiple stories describing their nightmarish ordeal.

Meanwhile, a seemingly more minor domestic drama was playing out at 39 Vanauley Street.

Fourteen-year-old Ron Moffatt had decided to run away from home—sort of—to escape punishment from playing hooky from school. As Moffatt would soon discover, this act of teenage defiance could not have possibly come at a worse time.

Ronald Clifton Moffatt was born April 24, 1942 to Omar and Bette Moffatt. His parents subsequently had two more boys. The family moved around a lot, but by the mid-1950s, had settled into the Vanauley Street area in downtown Toronto.

The 1954 City of Toronto directory identifies one "Omar Moffat" (spelled with one 't') residing at "39 Vanauley – 2" and working at "Moffats". The latter was the Moffat Stove Company in the Weston neighbourhood, where Omar toiled as a punch-press operator. Despite the similarity in names, there was no connection between the Moffatt family and Omar's place of work. That didn't, however, stop Omar's co-workers from teasing him about the strange coincidence.

The 1955 Toronto directory lists "Omer Moffel" at 39 Vanauley – 2. The directory for the following year uses the same incorrect spelling, at the same address. The 1957 directory gets half of the father's name right, identifying him as "Omer Moffatt" living at "39 Vanauley Street – h2".

Vanauley Street is in the lower part of what is now the Kensington-Chinatown neighbourhood, a stretch of downtown Toronto bordered by Queen Street in the south, Bathurst Street in the west, University Avenue in the east and College Street in the north. Chinatown, as the name implies, has a high Asian population. Kensington Market is a formerly rough and ready immigrant neighbourhood turned trendy locale today.

Back in the 1950s, Toronto was still dominated by White Anglo-Saxon Protestants (WASPs). In the 1951 Census, almost three-quarters of Torontonians indicated they were Protestants of British heritage. It was considered a major breakthrough in 1955 when the city elected Nathan Phillips as its first Jewish mayor. While today Toronto is a multicultural metropolis, it was uptight and insular at the time. There remained large pockets of poverty—like the street Moffatt lived on.

"The neighbourhood on Vanauley consisted of older, two story homes that were rented out as unheated, cold water flats. Across the street from where we lived was a neighborhood confectionary store. We lived about two blocks north of Queen Street West and the favourite restaurant on the corner of our street and Queen was called Dagwood's (named after the famous cartoon character of that time). Their specialty was hamburgers," recalls Moffatt today.

The Dagwood Snack Bar, as it was officially known, was located at 430 Queen Street West.

Moffatt describes his old neighbourhood as "rough, although reasonably quiet."

On top of living in a less than prime locale, Moffatt's family was poor and beset by substance abuse.

"My mother was a very heavy drinker and my father finally joined her and turned into one. He would come home from work and my mother would be drunk (on cheap wine) and usually entertaining a bunch of other drunks. Needless to say this would usually cause a confrontation and my brothers and I would hide out in the bedroom. The weekends were usually a drunken party, starting on Friday evening and lasting through until Saturday night," states Moffatt.

Sometimes, the family's money ran out by midweek. There wouldn't be enough cash for groceries, much less streetcar fare for Omar. Moffatt's father would sometimes end up walking to and from work, from downtown Toronto to Weston where his employer was located. To obtain sufficient supplies, Bette Moffatt sometimes dispatched Ron to the Scott Mission on Bathurst Street or to a Salvation Army branch to acquire food or vouchers.

Some of the apartments Moffatt lived in as a boy lacked central heating. Instead, a coal/wood-burning stove was used for cooking and heating purposes. When living in such places, Moffatt would be sent out, hatchet in hand, to find wood to chop up to feed the stove. He became well-acquainted with the back of furniture and appliance stores, where empty cardboard crates were dumped. Back in the '50s, these crates often had wooden frames, which could be hacked up for fuel.

Still, Moffatt was a normal kid in many ways. As a child, he enjoyed checking out new toys at the downtown Eaton's department store. When he got a bit older, Moffatt started listening to the new music of the day, including Elvis Presley and especially, the Everly Brothers.

Moffatt got along with his fellow classmates at school

and his peers in the neighbourhood. Interestingly, given the era, many of his friends were black.

"Probably my very best friend in those days was a black kid named Simon. We were always together, and I used to go to his parents often after school. His parents were always nice to me and usually invited me to stay for supper," says Moffatt.

"There was no open prejudice in Canada in those days. It was there beneath the surface, but I didn't care. These kids were great with me and were true and faithful friends. I was never one to usually get into fights at school (actually I would try and get out of any physical confrontation if I could help it). However, if I got into one and if it was with more than one other kid or a bigger kid than me, one of my black friends would come to my aid," he continues.

Moffatt generally recorded low marks at school, except in art (in which he always received 'A's) and Social Studies. Math and English composition were difficult. His parents sometimes split up and he would live with his grandparents or an aunt and uncle in Scarborough. Moffatt appreciated these respites from home, because it meant he could eat and dress well for a change.

By the time he hit 14, Moffatt was around 5'9 in height, lanky and relatively athletic. He loved hockey, but was impeded by a poor sense of balance. He couldn't skate properly or—significantly—ride a bicycle.

"Even when I walk, I never walk in a straight line. However, I was good at track and field and always made the school team and two or three times made it to the divisional finals at Christie Pits. One time I got all the way to the city finals for hurdles and high jumping at the old CNE stadium. My other sport was boxing which I took up at the Police Kiwanis club. I actually won my division at a tournament at the Gerrard Boxing Club," Moffatt notes.

Looking back today, Moffatt describes himself as a "go-getter" who was always interested in working to make extra money—understandable given his circumstances.

"When I was old enough I started getting odd jobs after school. I sold newspapers on the corner, set-up pins in a bowling alley. Two enterprising fellows I hung around with used to take me with them during the winter months shoveling rich people's driveways and during the Christmas season we would hit all the apartment buildings north of the Danforth and sing Christmas carols. I think people were paying us just to get us away from their doors, as we couldn't sing a lick. It was nice to have my own money and I became quite independent. I was even able to help my parents out now and then," he states.

Not all of Moffatt's money-making activities were so benign. By the mid-1950s, Moffatt was spending a lot of time hanging around St. Lawrence Market, then as now, a bustling center filled with food and crafts booths in downtown Toronto. When Moffatt was around 12 or 13—he isn't sure of his exact age—an older boy around 16, convinced him to engage in some petty thievery. The pair hid in an upper-floor room and waited for the market to close. Then they began searching around for money or valuables.

"We got up in the office and found a cigar box with $350. He gave me $20. We had to tie a cord together to go out the window. It was on the second-floor. We're going down, and a watchman saw us and started chasing us. We got away, but they knew who I was," recalls Moffatt.

Moffatt had spent so much time at the market, he was recognizable to the staff who worked at the place, including security guards. Moffatt ended up in detention for "three or four days" then went to Juvenile Court, he states. Having never been in trouble with the law before, Moffatt was given probation. The older boy did not get caught. Naturally, Moffatt's parents were furious and that was the end of his early criminal capers.

By 1956, Moffatt seemed to have smartened up. That summer, he took a job at the CNE.

"I worked on a ride called the Rotor. The ride looks like the inside of an old washing-machine. People would enter the ride and stand against the wall. The ride would begin spinning then all of a sudden the floor would drop out and you would find yourself stuck to the wall. My job was to put on demonstrations for the public," he recalls.

Moffatt worked at the ride until Labour Day, then went back to school. Moffatt was enrolled in grade seven.

On September 15, 1956, the *Toronto Daily Star* ran blaring ads for a big "rock and roll show" scheduled later that month for Maple Leaf Gardens. Among the acts scheduled to appear were Bill Haley and the Comets, the Platters, Frankie Lymon and the Teenagers, Chuck Berry, Shirley Lee, etc. The big movies in town that day included *The King and I* with Deborah Kerr and Yul Brynner and *High Society* with Bing Cosby, Grace Kelly and Frank Sinatra.

That evening, however, Moffatt was content to attend the Metro to watch two prior-run releases, *Ulysses* and *The Last Hunt*.

"The evening of the murder, I was watching movies at [the Metro] movie theatre, sitting with my friend's girlfriend," Moffatt recalls.

The friend in question was an usher at the Metro.

The manager of the Metro Theatre would later provide authorities with the precise run-times of all the films shown at his venue on Saturday, September 15. The second showing of the evening began with *Ulysses*, which ran from 5:30 p.m. until 7:15 p.m. *The Last Hunt* apparently started almost immediately after, at 7:15 p.m. and ran until 9:00 p.m. There was a cartoon ("Bone Sweet Bone") that lasted for 10 minutes. Then, inexplicably, an "Intermission" was scheduled between 9:10 and 9:15 p.m., after which, the second show for the night was over.

"I remember *Ulysses*. I used to love Kirk Douglas as an actor ... and [*The Last Hunt*] I remember Robert Taylor at the end of the movie frozen to death in a cave," recalls Moffatt today.

After staying the night at a friend's house, Moffatt

returned to his family apartment on the morning of Sunday, September 16. On Monday, at 5:30 a.m., with the death of Wayne Mallette all over the news, Moffatt woke up and headed to Odgen Public School on Phoebe Street (some accounts mistakenly stated that Moffatt attended a public school called Ryerson). He only attended class in the morning, however, electing to skip school in the afternoon. Newspapers would later speculate he was too nervous to stay in class because he had murdered little Wayne Mallette.

The same day Moffatt skipped school, the *Globe* ran a photograph showing where little Wayne Mallette's body was found on the CNE grounds: "It is right alongside the [rail-line] right-of-way through the CNE grounds; base of Hydro towers is at left," read the cutline to the picture.

Next to the crime scene photo was a shot of John Mallette, the boy's horrified looking father.

Tuesday, September 18, began in an unpleasant fashion. After getting up at 5:30 a.m., Moffatt was greeted by his father, who had found out his son had been playing hooky. Omar informed Ron that the two would speak later that day. Fearing his father's wrath, Moffatt came up with a plan. Not a very good plan, as these things go. After his father departed for work, Moffatt gathered up clothes and supplies and decided to run away—from the family apartment at least.

This was unusual behaviour for the boy, who had previously only made one, childhood attempt at running away from home. This attempt occurred when Moffatt was very young (he doesn't recall the exact age). He ended up wandering around in downtown Toronto, terrified at the sight of all the tall office buildings. Moffatt doesn't remember how he got back home, though presumably he was rescued by a Good Samaritan.

Moffatt's subsequent attempt at leaving home was considerably more deliberate. With his spare clothes and some food, Moffatt squirrelled himself into a hiding spot at 39 Vanauley. There is some discrepancy over the exact location of his hideout. Newspapers would place the spot in a closet cupboard in the basement. Moffatt, however, says he was actually hiding in "the first floor hall closet, downstairs from my parents' apartment."

Regardless, Moffatt's mother soon discovered her son hadn't gone to school. When Ron didn't come home for supper, Bette Moffatt contacted the Claremont Street police station to report her son missing.

A Toronto City Police Missing Person Report cited "family indifference" as the reason for Moffatt's absence. The document stated that Moffatt was last seen by his father early September 18, with clothing and food. The "Probable Destination" of the teenager is listed as "unknown".

Moffatt didn't return that night or the next. He established a pattern. He would hide out in his cubbyhole during the day, then work 4 – 11 p.m. at the Cozy Bowling Alley, where he had a part-time job. He took his meals at local restaurants. Still afraid to face his father, Moffatt didn't contact his parents. It was a fateful mistake.

In their search for the mysterious boy on the bicycle, Toronto police were checking all reports of runaway boys, aged 14 – 18. Authorities believed the suspect in the Wayne Mallette murder might have gone into hiding.

A police teletype message alerted authorities that Moffatt was missing. The teletype gave his name and description, stating, he was "male white, 14 years, 5/6 ½", 150 pounds, med bld brown hair, brn eyes, good teeth, Canadian ... wearing light blue jeans, pink silk shirt, red socks, black shoes, rust coloured windbreaker." Someone hand wrote "ruddy comp" and "str hair" on one these teletype messages. The note contained a few mistakes concerning Moffatt's physical details. Moffatt's father is named "Omer" and his mother "Betty" in the same script.

The investigation into the Mallette murder was taking top priority, however.

On September 20, the Toronto Police Commission announced a $2,000 reward "to be paid for information leading to the arrest or conviction of the person or persons responsible for the death of Wayne Mallette," as the official release put it. The same day, Wayne Mallette was buried in his hometown of Seeley's Bay.

Police investigated a range of teenagers who might have been involved with the crime. The boys were usually singled out because they were either known to police, frequented the CNE or were fond of riding bicycles. A police memo, dated September 16, referred to one such suspect as "a fast-talking punk who hangs around the C.N.E. with a bicycle." The boy's name was given, and his age (14) and address. A handwritten follow-up citation underlined the boy's name and said, "Checked O.K. Sept. 18". The same memo included a list of schools to check and mentioned an interview with Exhibition watchman, George Sinclair. "THERE IS LITTLE DOUBT THE YOUTH HE WAS TALKING TO IS OUR BOY" stated an all-caps line in the note.

Another memo, written by the same officer and from September 17, mentioned two girls, both aged 10, who had apparently seen "a youth with a bicycle, who answered to the description" of the mystery cyclist. "We interviewed [a witness], who says that she and other girls have seen this boy on several occasions, in or near the C.N.E., and at the lakeshore. He stares at them, and on one occasion makes some indecent suggestion," stated the memo. It might have been coincidence, but the description certainly fit with the activities of Peter Woodcock.

Woodcock, however, wasn't even on the police radar. Authorities were, however, starting to set their sights on Ron Moffatt. The more they checked into Moffatt's background, the more he seemed like a prime suspect. Not only was Moffatt roughly the same age as the mysterious cyclist, he had been an employee at the Ex and was intimately familiar with the CNE grounds. It would be a natural place for him to hang out, even after the Exhibition closed. And of course, there was the matter of Moffatt's disappearance, the timing of which seemed deeply suspicious. Authorities soon found their suspect.

On Friday, September 21, Inspector Payne and Det. Simmonds, the officer who had been present at the Mallette crime scene and autopsy, visited 39 Vanauley Street. Around 11:30 a.m., they interviewed Bette Moffatt in her apartment. Ms. Moffatt had no idea her son was hiding in her own building, much less that Toronto Police now considered him a potential murderer.

Authorities had been alerted by a local storekeeper that the missing Moffatt boy had been seen entering and leaving 39 Vanauley Street on a few occasions. After talking to Bette Moffatt, the visiting officers looked around the area. At 12:20 p.m., the pair walked back inside 39 Vanauley, went downstairs and began a close inspection. About 25 minutes into their search, the pair noticed a closet under a stairway. Police opened the closet and there inside, asleep under a blanket, was Ron Moffatt. He had no idea who these two men were who had uncovered his hiding spot. Moffatt was terrified.

Inspector Payne was "a big scary man ... [the two policemen] said, 'Come with us.' I thought they were truant officers," he recalls.

The boy was placed in the back of a squad car. He was whisked off to the College Street police station. Moffatt buried his hands in his face as the car drove away. His parents were not notified that their boy had been found.

A subsequent memo from Detective Simmonds offered the police side of things:

"He had his hands over his face and appeared to be

either crying, or possibly was not quite awake or else the bright light was hurting his eyes. Inspector Payne asked him what was the trouble and he replied to the effect, 'I couldn't stand it any more, I had to do something, saying something about a fight that occurred in the house and either his mother or father throwing water at someone. Payne then said, 'It's what happened at the Exhibition Ground that we are talking about – Were you down at the Ex?' and he replied "Yes"," wrote Det. Simmonds.

The comment about throwing water was a reference to a recent argument Ron had with his mother. The argument had climaxed when Bette Moffatt threw a saucepan of water at her son.

Police arrived at the College Street station around 1 p.m. Ten minutes later, Moffatt found himself in an interrogation room with Inspector Payne and Detective Simmonds.

"Inspector Payne asked him certain questions, as to age, what school he was attending, when he was at school last, he said he was last at school Monday, he said he was good at Art, that he got along well at home. He said he did not own a bicycle, but that he borrowed a wheel once in a while," continued Det. Simmonds' memo.

Moffatt was asked about his work history. He told police he'd worked at the Rotor ride at "the Ex" as well as a bowling alley and car wash. Payne and Simmonds weren't interested in his other part-time jobs, but zeroed in on Moffatt's familiarity with the CNE.

"He was asked if he was around the Ex last Saturday

and he said Yes, I went down around the Rotor. When asked what he was doing at the Ex, he stated: 'I was fooling around, I go down there a lot,'" read the memo.

The memo sends up an immediate red flag: Moffatt insists he was incapable of riding a bike. Other factors were also overlooked. Moffatt was taller than Peter Woodcock and had been wearing a pink shirt for the past several days (while the bicyclist spotted by the night watchman wore a white t-shirt with red stripes in a horizontal pattern). Moffatt had a windbreaker, but it wasn't grey. Rather, it was the colour of rust. Even the earlier police teletype had noted these clothing choices.

Moffatt was instructed to stand up and open his shirt. Police noticed a mark on his shoulder. When the boy took his pants down, it was observed he had an abrasion on his right hip, about one-and-a-half inches in diameter. Moffatt apparently shrugged when he asked how he got this abrasion.

The interrogation continued.

From the memo:

"Q. You haven't explained to us, was there anything else happened at the Exhibition grounds last Saturday you haven't told us about?"

(Moffatt): (No answer)

Q. Were you in a fight with a boy in the Exhibition Grounds?

(Moffatt): A boy was bothering me, he wouldn't leave me alone, I chased him and grabbed him, I shoved his head down into the dirt and when he didn't move, I got scared."

After this dramatic admission, Moffatt's interrogators apparently paused, as per police procedure.

"Inspector Payne said at this time, "Just a minute, Ron, the way this thing is going now, it's only fair to let you know that you are going to be charged with Murder [,"] and he started to say something and Pay[n]e stopped him and I typed a heading on a caution sheet that I had placed in the typewriter. Inspector Payne got up from the chair he was sitting in beside the accused and took a stand beside me and read the caution to the accused … the accused said anything you want to know I'll tell you and from that point on I typed everything that was said," stated Det. Simmonds' memo.

At the top of Moffatt's confession are the type-written words, "You are arrested on a charge of the murder of Wayne Mallette, 7 years of age, Saturday, Sept. 15, 1956 at Canadian National Exhibition." This is followed by the text of the caution Det. Payne referred to, pre-printed on the page. The caution read: "Do you wish to say anything in answer to the charge? You are not obliged to say anything unless you wish to do so, but whatever you say will be taken down in writing and may be given in evidence."

Then, as now, it was not mandatory for a lawyer or parent to be present during these hearings, despite the age of the accused.

Moffatt's memory of the interrogation centers less

on police procedure and more on raw intimidation. He recalls being badgered insistently, being told he was a murderer. The 14-year-old runaway wasn't physically abused, but the threat was in the air.

"They played good cop, bad cop. [Det. Simmonds] was the good cop and Payne was the bad cop. He would grab me and say, 'You'd better start talking or things are going to get rough here.' You're a 14-year-old kid, and this big galoot has you," Moffatt recalls today.

This went on for some time. In addition to their threats and intensity, police threw out very leading questions to the scared boy.

"They walked me through the confession, supplying the correct information when I gave them a wrong answer to a question etc.," states Moffatt.

On the face of it, Moffatt's confession was both lurid and convincing.

Moffatt told police that on September 15, he stole a bicycle and rode to the deserted Exhibition Place, to hang out at his old stomping grounds. He helped a man unload a truck then rode to an area and sat down. That's when a little boy—Wayne Mallette—approached and started annoying him.

"I told him to go away and he wouldn't pay attention to me, he kicked me, I got up and started to fight with him, I got my arm on his neck and I put a bit too much pressure on, I got up, and I spoke to him and he didn't answer, I was scared so I moved his body, then I took the bike and I headed for the Princes' Gate," stated Moffatt, in his confession.

He met a watchman near the Pure Food Building, asked about finding bodies in the bushes then departed on his bicycle.

"I went to behind the armouries near the railroad tracks that's where I put the bike there, amongst a bunch of small trees. Then I thought for a while what I'd do, I crossed the tracks, and over the bridge to Lakeshore Boulevard, walked to Bathurst and went up Bathurst along Queen to Johnny's restaurant, I had something to eat, and I went up to the Metro show to see if my boy friend was there, I asked the Assistant Manager, and he said he had gone home," continued the confession.

The boy friend—1950s slang for a male pal, not a partner or lover—was supposedly the teen who worked as an usher at the Metro. In his confession, Moffatt said he went to his friend's house, told him he was in trouble, and stayed the night there. On Monday, when he went to school, news of Mallette's murder was in the air, and Moffatt grew nervous police would catch him, so he gathered food and clothing and went into hiding.

"I kept on hanging around the Exhibition for the rest of the week. I slept in a closet downstairs where I live where you found me," stated the admission.

The confession, which was signed by Moffatt and Det. Simmonds, included some rather leading questions.

"Q. Did you have a bowel movement out beside where the body of Wayne Mallette was found?

(Moffatt): I had it right before he came in where I was. That's where I moved the body to after the fight."

And:

"Q. Why did you ask the watchman about seeing any bodies?

(Moffatt): I was scared they might have already found the body.

Q. When you told the watchman you saw another fellow that looked like your double, why was that done?"

(Moffatt): They might think it was me so I told them I had a double."

A modern interpretation might suggest police were feeding the boy details of the crime, but no matter. Authorities were convinced they had the right suspect. After finishing the confession, police gave Moffatt some food then drove him to the Exhibition grounds. Det. Simmonds and Inspector Payne took the boy through the Dufferin Gates where he allegedly showed them where he had been hanging around the day of the murder and where he encountered Wayne Mallette. At one point, police stopped the vehicle and began to walk around. During this crime scene tour, Moffatt supposedly furnished police with information about the killing. He told them where he had encountered the night watchman, the location of his escape route from the Ex, and where he ditched his stolen bike, state police records. No bicycle was found in the search.

Needless to say, there is considerable difference of opinion as to who was actually leading the tour. Police said Moffatt showed them around. Moffatt says the opposite.

"They led me directly to the crime scene. I had no clue as to its whereabouts. They would say, 'It was right over here that you left the body. Wasn't it?' and other things of that nature," says Moffatt.

Moffatt was returned to the station when the tour was over. Police notes indicate that Inspector Payne went to fetch Bette Moffatt shortly after 5:10 p.m. At 6:45 p.m., Moffatt was finally allowed to see his mother. According to police records, Bette Moffatt waited for her son in the office of Inspector John Nimmo. Ron Moffatt was brought in by Det. Simmonds. The police record stated that Moffatt sobbed and admitted to his mother (in front of police) that he had killed Wayne Mallette. Asked why, Moffatt "shook his head and said, "I don't know, we got into a fight, I didn't mean it," reported police.

Bette Moffatt would later complain bitterly it had taken police hours to tell them what had happened to their son, after Inspector Payne and Det. Simmonds dropped by 39 Vanauley Street.

"When my mother came to the police station after my interrogation, I was very distraught and in a state of panic and was afraid to tell her the truth that I was innocent for fear of going through another session with Payne in my face. Had I been assured that my mother would have been allowed in the interrogation room during further questioning I would have changed my story, but as far as I can recall, I was not assured of this," states Moffatt.

On Saturday, September 22, Inspector Payne and another officer also took Moffatt to the Dental College at the University of Toronto. There, authorities made casts of his teeth (to see if his mouth matched the bite marks on Mallette's leg). While at the dental office, authorities also took photographs of his various bruises and marks on his knees and hips. Moffatt was then driven back to the police station where he supposedly made another lurid confession.

"...he was then taken to Inspector Nimmo's office, where Inspector Payne asked him, "Ron, you no doubt know why we had the impression of your teeth taken, I am really interested in knowing why you bit this lad, and I am not going to caution you and I realize you may not want to answer this, that you may feel embarrassed but I think it is important that we know just why you bit this lad. Can you tell us any reason for this?" stated a memo from Inspector Payne.

According to the officer, Moffatt said, "I just get a feeling, it seems I like to bite flesh" and then "made a biting motion twice."

Today, Moffatt says his admission of guilt was all nonsense—the product of a very scared boy pushed into making a false confession. While almost entirely wrong about everything else, media coverage at the time did accurately reflect Moffatt's anguished emotional state.

"A terror-stricken 14-year-old boy, who hid for four days in a stairway cupboard next door to his Vanauley St. home, is under arrest in connection with the suffocation death of Wayne Richard Mallette, seven, of Seeleys

Bay, whose body was found last Sunday in a clump of bushes at the CNE ... The boy worked at the CNE midway on the roto-scooter, according to his mother ... Because the boy is held as a juvenile delinquent for an appearance before Judge V. Lorne Stewart, his name was not disclosed. Crown Attorney Henry H. Bull said he didn't know what procedure would be taken but other officials said it would be likely the boy would be charged with murder," read a September 22, 1956 story in the *Toronto Daily Star*.

Given the terrible situation Ron Moffatt now found himself in, the fact his name was being kept out of the papers because he was a juvenile was perhaps his only consolation.

Chapter Two - Misfit on a Bike

Ron Moffatt was brought before Juvenile Court Judge Lorne Stewart on Monday, September 24, 1956, three days after making his signed confession to police. Inspector Adolphus Payne and Sergeant of Detectives Bernard Simmonds discussed the case for over an hour with Crown Attorney William Gibson. Then, Judge Stewart announced the official charge: "That being a juvenile delinquent, [Ron Moffatt] did kill and slay one Wayne Mallette on Sept. 15."

Counsel for Moffatt entered a plea of not guilty. Despite his confession, there would be a full trial. The justice remanded Moffatt until October 1. Moffatt was taken to the Juvenile Detention Centre on Christie Street.

Moffatt was booked as juvenile delinquent, not an adult. This was hugely significant, although it's doubtful that the terrified Moffatt would have appreciated the legal distinction at the time. An adult facing a murder charge could be put to death if convicted. Capital punishment was still in effect, not to be officially abolished by the Canadian government until decades later. Juvenile delinquents, however, did not face the death penalty. Moffatt wasn't entirely off-the-hook, however; Judge Stewart had the authority to move the trial to adult court if he felt circumstances warranted it

A *Toronto Daily Star* article covering Moffatt's court appearance described him as "a nice looking boy, he wore a pinkish coloured shirt under a sweater."

Such details were more important than they seemed. Besides the fact Moffatt was taller than the real killer and didn't wear glasses, no one ever described Peter Woodcock as handsome, much less stylish.

Police, however, were convinced they had the right suspect. Their blinkered vision was partly a reflection of the fact Toronto cops simply didn't have much experience dealing with murder cases. The Boyd Gang aside, Toronto wasn't a particularly wild or violent place at the time. In 1956, there were nine recorded murders in the city, down from 11 the year before, according to a report to the Board of Commissioners of Police. Three additional manslaughter cases in 1956 brought the total number of reported criminal deaths in the city to a dozen. By way of comparison, Toronto today (admittedly bigger, but still quite a safe city) recorded 74 homicides in 2016.

The entire country was relatively peaceful. There were 171 criminal homicide deaths recorded nationwide in 1956, according to Statistics Canada. Of this total, a mere two-dozen murder cases made it to court that year, in a nation of 16 million people.

Police were convinced of Moffatt's guilt, however. So were certain members of the public, such as the concerned citizen—who shall remain nameless—who wrote a note addressed to "Chief Constable John Chisholm" claiming the reward money for information leading to the capture of Mallette's killer.

"I wish to advise that I am the person who gave the information to the whereabouts of the person charged with the above death to the arresting Police Officers," read the neatly typed note, dated September 27, 1956.

Moffatt's parents, however, loudly protested their boy's innocence. In a front-page story in the *Toronto Daily Star* on September 22, Omar and Bette Moffatt accused police of making a huge mistake. Moffatt's family life might been largely dysfunctional, but following his arrest, his parents stood by their son. Their support came as a pleasant surprise to Moffatt.

"Shocked and angry, the 32-year-old mother of the 14-year-old lad arrested in connection with the slaying of Wayne Mallette, seven, said today: 'My boy is a good boy. Why, he cried like a baby when I saw him in police custody.' ... The boy's father, 36, a Weston factory worker, said, 'I don't think he was involved in a murder.' ... neighbours of the family in the Queen St.-Spadina Ave. area said: 'That family was awfully strict with their boy.' .... The dark-haired mother of the lad, who has two other children—one an eight-month-old-baby said, 'My son is innocent, until he is proven guilty,' read the article.

Bette Moffatt also noted her son once lost a job at a

corner store "because he couldn't even ride a bicycle properly."

Peter Woodcock, by contrast, could ride a bike. It was one of the few athletic endeavours he engaged in. His choice of wheels was "a red racing bike, with hand brakes, the right-hand brake broken, square battery light on the handle bars, white fenders with two reflector tapes on them," wrote the *Toronto Daily Star*. Woodcock took this racing bike all over the city and into the countryside. He rode in warm and cold weather alike, to explore and find children to molest.

Woodcock was an odd duck, to put it mildly. He was short, about 5'6, and slight, weighing only around 100 pounds. His hair was dark, his face was pimply and he wore horn-rimmed glasses to see properly. Woodcock was enrolled in grade 11 at Bloordale College, a private school. He lived on wealthy Lytton Boulevard in north Toronto with foster parents, Frank and Susan Maynard. His foster father worked as an accountant.

While much about Woodcock's motivations remains unknown, the basic contours of his life have been well-documented.

"Born in March of 1939, Peter began life with all the cards stacked against him," read a rather melodramatic profile of Woodcock in the January 22, 1957 *Star*.

The *Star* piece focused on the multiple physical maladies Woodcock suffered as a child. These included a twisted neck, which was operated on when Woodcock was an infant, an enlarged thymus and a malformed ear, fixed in another operation when the boy was six. He also had a droopy eye and suffered bronchitis and other respiratory ailments when growing up.

This description, however, only covered part of Woodcock's troubles.

In a book about Woodcock, crime author Mark Bourrie described the boy as "a strange, fussing baby born out of wedlock" to a teenage mother, who was either a prostitute or factory worker.

An article in the April 11, 1957 *Globe and Mail* said Woodcock's birth mother was 17 years-old and herself illegitimate.

His father was supposedly a soldier, though that's not clear. In either case, neither of Woodcock's parents were interested in looking after him. As an infant, Woodcock was surrendered to Children's Aid and bounced around a series of foster homes. Little Woodcock didn't endear himself to any of his temporary parents.

"He screamed constantly and wouldn't eat. The baby's crying never stopped so the Children's Aid moved him from one set of foster parents to another. He never slept, he never ate, and no one could stand to be near him," wrote Bourrie.

Woodcock expressed terror when people got too physically close for his comfort. He didn't begin talking until around age two. When he did talk, he was shrill and incomprehensible. He was unloved and unwanted.

When Woodcock reached three, amazingly enough, he was placed in a family that did want him. The Maynards were a comfortable, upper-middle class couple with one boy of their own. During the Second World War, Frank and Susan Maynard regularly took in low-income children or orphans, looking after them until they could be adopted by other families.

In later court proceedings, Mrs. Maynard described her foster son as "the most pathetic little soul you ever saw." She also described him as "afflicted with fears and nervous ailments" and a "sickly" child who "lacked co-ordination," noted the April 11, 1957 *Globe*.

It is unclear why the Maynards were so devoted to Woodcock, though the *Globe* court coverage did quote his foster mother as stating, "If anyone needed a home and love, he did."

That said, the Children's Aid Society recommended against formally adopting Woodcock. The Maynards followed this advice and never did adopt the boy, who remained a ward of Children's Aid until he turned 18. The family did, however, shower their strange foster son with affection and creature comforts. When Woodcock was 10 years old, the Maynards moved to a large, elegant home on Lytton Boulevard in one of Toronto's nicer neighbourhoods.

If the Maynards thought Woodcock might grow out of his toddler eccentricities they were wrong. The boy grew up to be eccentric and unsociable. He had no friends his own age and was either ignored or bullied by other kids. He was small, weak and non-athletic. His school experiences were uniformly awful.

In court, Mrs. Maynard said Woodcock's "first few years in kindergarten and public school were miserable," wrote the *Globe*.

The Maynards did their best to help, taking Woodcock to a wide array of doctors and specialists. He was removed from public school and placed in a private academy called Waycroft School, but didn't fare much better there.

When he was seven, the Maynards entered their foster son in a treatment program at the Hospital for Sick Children to alter his strange behaviour. He remained in treatment for years, without much improvement. Woodcock's strange behaviours included a tendency to disappear. As a child, he wandered frequently, sometimes not coming home at all at night, prompting frantic searches on the part of his foster family. He had a habit of slashing his clothing and carving patterns into the family dining room table. He was the chief suspect in the death of his mother's canary. Susan Maynard had left her home briefly. Upon returning, she discovered her pet bird, dead. The canary corpse was lying on the piano, with candles around its prone body, wrote Bourrie. Of course, Woodcock denied killing the bird, blaming its death on the family dog.

There were other disturbing auguries. After Woodcock became notorious, the *Globe* ran an article referencing an incident from 1950, when a Children's Aid social worker named Elspeth Lattimer took Woodcock to the Canadian National Exhibition. It was a grimly ironic choice, given Woodcock would later commit his first documented murder there. At the time, Woodcock unnerved his social worker by telling her how much he hated the other kids running about. According to Lattimer, Woodcock said he hoped a bomb "would fall and kill all the children."

In 1951, it was decided that Woodcock would benefit from full-time institutional care. He spent three years in the Sunnyside Children's Centre, located in Kingston, Ontario. This facility offered around the clock care and supervision for problem children.

Woodcock returned home to see his foster family for vacations. While in Kingston, Woodcock served in the Sea Cadets. If his own account can be believed, he was entrusted with guard duty, complete with loaded rifle. Woodcock was released back to the Maynard's care in 1954, supposedly ready to make his way in regular society. He went to Lawrence Park Collegiate Institute, but for less than two months. As before, Woodcock was regularly bullied and harassed by his classmates. He later attended Bloordale College.

While Woodcock was a social misfit with his peers, he excelled in other areas and was precocious for his age. He preferred to read news magazines to comics, and was more interested in astronomy and politics than sports. He had no interest in rock and roll or popular music in general, preferring the classics. Woodcock did highly value his bike, however.

"Peter's prize possession was his bicycle," stated the January 22, 1957 *Star*, quoting a Sunnyside official who said, "He's had it ever since he returned from Kingston and takes good care of it."

Indeed, once he got back from Kingston, Woodcock started taking long rides around city streets and rural locales. He also enjoyed riding on public transit by himself—a habit he had developed as a young child. As a little boy, he would regularly stowaway on city buses and streetcars which sometimes took him far outside the city borders. This solitary teen, who preferred classical music to pop, also had an extremely vivid fantasy life.

Sometimes as he rode his bike, Woodcock fantasized about being on missions, leading something called the "Winchester Heights Gang"—an imaginary collection of 500 "invisible but obedient boys" as Bourrie put it in his book. Being head of this fantasy gang made the largely powerless Woodcock feel powerful and in control.

Like most adolescents, he thought at length about sex. When it came to performing sex acts, however, Woodcock preferred to gratify himself with children, not partners his age. He would later tell police he had molested a series of children without being caught. His modus operandi was to approach young kids on his bicycle and engage them in conversation. The kids were often fascinated by his fancy looking bike. When Woodcock offered to give them a ride on his handlebars, many of them took him up on the offer. Woodcock's vile luring technique would later be corroborated by witnesses.

Woodcock benefitted from the social mores of the day.

The 1950s were a more trusting era, in which "stranger danger" was not yet on the radar of most parents. Kids typically played outside, unsupervised by adults.

Woodcock would take children into secluded locales, such as the Don Valley. The latter was a wild area in the center of the city, filled with trees, bushes and hiding spots. Then, and now, Toronto has plenty of lonely wooded spots and ravines. In such places, Woodcock sexually molested the little kids he picked up.

Woodcock's sexual antics started off in nonviolent fashion—or as nonviolent as molesting innocent kids can be. Woodcock gradually gave vent to his more sadistic impulses, however, and began choking his victims, sometimes to the point they went unconscious. Once the children had passed out, Woodcock would take off on his bicycle, leaving his victims to wake up, unclothed and sexually abused, in secluded locales.

This activity did not go unnoticed. Woodcock had a close call with police in this period. If the incident in question had been taken more seriously and Woodcock punished properly, a series of future crimes might never had occurred.

The incident involved a young girl whom Woodcock decided to murder.

"I wanted to go to the next phase [of criminality] ... There was a 10 year-old girl. I did have plans to cut her to see what she looked like inside," Woodcock explained to author Bourrie.

Woodcock told Bourrie he wanted to perform "a very thorough anatomical lesson" on the girl.

Woodcock arranged to meet the girl in the Don Valley, to carry this plan through. Woodcock identified the time period as March 1956, but police and newspaper accounts pin the event as taking place in June. Regardless of the exact date, Woodcock armed himself with a penknife (which he assumed would be up to the task of murder and dissection) and met the girl in the Don Valley. He did not, however, kill her. This was partly due to the fact it was getting dark and Woodcock feared being lost in the dense, wooded Valley at night. It's also likely he simply couldn't summon the nerve to carry through with his plans. The pair tromped around for hours then finally climbed out of the Valley.

The girl's parents, meanwhile, reported to police that she had been kidnapped. North York police officers searched unsuccessfully for her. After hours of fruitless searching by authorities, the girl phoned her parents and announced she hadn't been kidnapped after all, but was in fact in a phone booth around Bayview Avenue and Blythwood Road.

Four lawmen, led by Sgt. Arthur Stevens rushed to the spot. They found the girl inside the phone booth, with Woodcock.

A subsequent account appearing months later in the *Toronto Daily Star* stated that police "took the pair to the station and after learning the girl had not been molested, they released Woodcock after Sgt. Stevens had given him a severe lecture."

Police also paid a visit to Woodcock's foster family. Unsurprisingly, Mrs. Maynard was very upset, both by her foster child's action and the presence of a police car outside her genteel home. Once police left, Woodcock began arguing with his parents. He threatened to commit suicide, which led to an even more heated row. After his mother stomped off, Mr. Maynard quietly ordered Woodcock not to bother any more kids.

The incident with the young girl remained largely forgotten, until Woodcock appeared once more on police radar a few months later.

There was another incident too that sounded very much like the actions of Woodcock. A police memo titled "RE: W.R. MALLETTE" cited an interview authorities conducted September 19, 1956 with a concerned mother. She told police about a strange encounter between her son and a teenage boy. Dennis, who was three-and-a-half, had been playing outside on the afternoon of September 7 when he briefly disappeared. Around 4:30 p.m., a teenage boy, described in the memo as "16 yrs, 5'8", dark hair, medium complexion, wearing a baseball cap and a sweater with long sleeves and a crest" delivered Dennis home. The boy claimed he found the child wandering around High Park, then left.

The mother noticed her son "looked dazed" and had injuries—a bump on the back of the head, abrasions, red marks on his neck and scratches. There were bite marks on his stomach. The startled parents questioned Dennis who said "a boy had come along while he was playing and had walked him along the new roadway to some bushes ... where he had tied his hands behind his back with some rope or string; had tied some rope or string around his neck; had punched him on the back and he told his mother that the boy had a large "dodo" his word for penis," read the memo.

The boy was taken to hospital where his injuries were confirmed. Doctors said the scratches on Dennis' neck were "consistent with marks that would be made by thin rope or string around the throat. The teeth marks were clearly marked although they did not break the skin. [Doctors] did not examine the boy for a criminal assault and so could not offer an opinion as to whether the boy had been sexually assaulted or not. The lump and abrasions on the back of the boys' head would be consistent with a fall or a blow," stated the memo.

The identity of the assailant was never confirmed, though the incident perfectly fits Peter Woodcock's standard approach and choice of helpless, young victim.

Woodcock wasn't entirely fixated on attacking children, however. In 1956, he engaged in one of normal rites of passage for most teenagers: he got a summer job. Woodcock worked at Casa Loma, a huge home built by a Toronto businessman to resemble a castle. Casa Loma is a big tourist draw, and it was Woodcock's job to direct the cars of visitors into the parking lot. In his spare time, he cycled around the city, looking for kids.

Chapter Three – A Death at Cherry Beach

On the afternoon of Saturday, October 6, 1956, nine-year-old Gary Morris and his friend, eight-year-old William Christie, went to see a matinee at the Regent movie theatre at Queen and Sherbourne Streets in downtown Toronto. The kids left before the show ended and hung out on the street for a while. They collected some empty soda bottles and exchanged these for candy bars, elastic bands and paper clips. They returned to Morris' house at 304 ½ Queen Street East, got some apples, then stood outside the residence, chatting. Around 3:30 p.m., the boys were approached by "an unknown youth on a bicycle" as a subsequent police report put it.

Morris crossed the street and began talking to the stranger, who looked around 14 – 18 years old and wore a windbreaker with blue jeans. He had dark hair and glasses. His bike was red and the right-hand brake seemed broken.

Christie later told police that Morris and the stranger chatted about shooting pigeons at Cherry Beach on

Toronto's waterfront. At the time, Cherry Beach was a dismal stretch of wasteland by Lake Ontario. An October 11, *Globe and Mail* article called it a "shabby sandy beach" with a "history of crime" including "murders and muggings, rapes and petty thievery." The article spoke of reports about a knife-point rape at the beach and several young men who had been mugged there.

It's unclear how much Morris knew about Cherry Beach's bad reputation, or cared. The boy on the bike said he too was heading to Cherry Beach. Perhaps Morris would like a ride on his handlebars? The little boy eagerly agreed and hopped on and the two biked away. It was the last time Christie saw his friend alive.

The stranger headed to Cherry Beach, as promised. Only instead of hunting pigeons, the teen turned his attentions to his young passenger. The teenager strangled Morris until he passed out. Then he removed the boy's clothes and examined him. Examination complete, the youthful predator attacked the child, biting and jumping on him. When he had enough, the assailant left Morris for dead and vanished from the scene on his bike.

Around 8:15 p.m. that evening, Irene Morris, reported her son was missing. Police commenced a search. On the morning of October 10, a patrol of 30 cops led by Inspector Samuel Johnson, checked Cherry Beach for any sign of the boy. Their mission was made more difficult by tall, uncut grass, untrimmed bushes and prolific weeds. The area was also filled with rubbish. Two weeks prior to Morris' disappearance, Toronto authorities voted to spend around $10,000 to clean up the weeds and garbage at Cherry Beach to satisfy the demands of local residents. The jungle-like environment was so bad, the search party might have passed Morris several times before locating him.

Around 8:30 a.m., a constable named William Bushell found the boy in a clump of bushes. At first, police thought the child was just sleeping. There was no pulse and the boy's skin was cold. Constables found "paper clips and rubber bands, as well as three T.T.C. car tickets" in Morris' pants pocket, stated a police report. The search party also found bite marks on the boy's neck.

Photographs were taken of the bite marks on Morris' body. The boy was removed from the scene and taken to a coroner's office. There, the body was identified by his father, Charles Morris.

Chief Coroner Dr. Smirlie Lawson autopsied the boy around 11:15 a.m. The Coroner told reporters Morris had likely been murdered in one spot then moved to another. Gary had suffered terrible injuries, including a ruptured liver (which might have alone been fatal). It was speculated the killer jumped on the victim's body several times, landing with his knees on the boy's back. The kind of move a professional wrestler might make, except in this case the violence was real. Gary Morris didn't die from this torture, however. His death came from asphyxiation. It was possible the assailant had smothered his victim by lying on top on him, making it impossible to breath.

The brutal assault shocked police.

"Teeth marks and a ruptured liver are evidence of a sadistic attack," stated Chief of Detectives Archie McCathie, as reported by the October 11 *Toronto Daily Star*.

Police said the attack wasn't sexual in nature ("He had not been sexually attacked," read a police report). In reality, police did think sex was involved. Authorities interviewed several known sex offenders with histories of molesting boys. None of the interviews were helpful in any way.

Gary's parents expressed shock and bewilderment. As far as Charles and Irene Morris were aware, Gary never expressed any interest in killing birds or going to Cherry Beach, which wasn't exactly a prime spot for kids to play.

For the second time in less than a month, a little child had been abducted and killed by a mysterious teenager on a bicycle. Once again, police went to local schools to inspect bike racks. Kids with red racing bikes, the kind Christie observed, were questioned.

"The boy on the bicycle is the last one known to have seen Gary alive," reported the October 11 *Star*, adding, "After Mallette was found dead, a youth on a bicycle was hunted until detectives found the Vanauley Street suspect who had left home, hiding in a stairway cupboard near his home."

Impressions were made of the bite marks left on Morris. These were compared to the bite marks left on Mallette. Authorities declared that the dental patterns didn't match. This seemed proof that "the Mallette boy's death [was not] connected with the current murder," wrote the *Star*.

This shaky forensic evidence was indicative of the confused nature of the investigation. The city's nickname at the time was "Toronto the Good" and the police department's lack of experience with homicide led to some strange conclusions. An unnamed police source in the October 11 *Globe* suggested that "a psychopathic person might have read of [Mallette's] slaying and the power of suggestion might have prompted him to kill Gary Morris."

Essentially, police were saying that two different teenage boys had killed a child in the same city, barely weeks apart. And both suspects just happened to ride bicycles. It apparently hadn't dawned on anyone that a single, bike-riding killer was responsible for both deaths. And that the killer in question was not Ron Moffatt, currently in detention.

Such obliviousness worked greatly to Peter Woodcock's advantage.

Murdering Gary Morris had not been a spontaneous decision. In fact, Woodcock had started thinking about committing another atrocity almost immediately after killing Wayne Mallette.

His first order of business had been to find a new killing site. Through his bike trips, Woodcock was well-acquainted with lonely, isolated locales within the city. Little visited Cherry Beach seemed the perfect place to commit a murder. After settling on a crime scene, Woodcock scouted around for a fresh victim, preferably another small, helpless boy. He found Gary Morris and abducted him. After abusing the child, he killed him then pedalled away. Despite having committed two murders, Woodcock remained above suspicion.

Decades later, Moffatt still can't believe how blind police were when it came to investigating the Gary Morris murder

"The most startling part is: (one) a boy on a bicycle was involved and (two) the second victim was bitten just the same way as Wayne Mallette was. Here is the kicker—they mention about me being in custody for the first murder and that they took my dental impressions and matched them up to the second victim's bite marks and said that they did not match. Instead of alarm bells going off and thinking, 'Maybe we have the wrong person in custody' they instead decide they have a second person running around killing children using the same method of killing. Unbelievable," says Moffatt.

The *Annual Report of the Chief Constable* for 1956 given to Toronto's Board of Commissioners of Police, detailed all nine of the city's recorded murder cases that year. Wayne Mallette and Gary Morris are listed on the same page. The report noted the boys' youth (Wayne was seven, Gary nine) and the fact both kids were found in isolated locations. The report discussed how both boys died (asphyxiation) but differed greatly when it came to the outcome of the cases. The entry on Mallette noted that "one Ronald Moffatt, 14 years, was apprehended" and quickly confessed to murdering Mallette (the report used Moffatt's full name, though that detail was kept from the newspapers). The entry about Morris, by contrast, reported the boy had last been seen with a mysterious bicycle-riding youth but that police hadn't solved the case.

Needless to say, officials had no plans to release Moffatt from the Juvenile Detention Centre on Christie Street.

Moffatt has strong memories of the place: "the facility was located in a rather large house on the west side of Christie Street... There was a very large common room where we had our meals and spent most of the day, reading, playing cards etc. There was no television; however, a radio was turned on now and then. Off of the common room was located a room used as a classroom. It was compulsory for all residents to attend class. As I recall, there was no actual teaching of Math, English, etc. Instead most of the day was spent doing art projects or reading or listening to music."

"The facility had both a boys and girls section. We were only allowed to socialize with the opposite sex during the classroom sessions (needless to say nobody ever tried to get out of going to school). The only other time we saw the girls was at meal time, but we were not allowed to talk with them. Everyone slept in dormitories. The girls used to come in during the day to make our beds, so the boys would leave notes under their pillows to communicate their interest in a certain girl or vice versa," continues Moffatt.

Meals were made on-site, in a fully-equipped kitchen.

Moffatt was chosen to do kitchen work and found himself washing a lot of dishes. A female cook was nice to him, and showed how to cook a few simple things like eggs. Food in general was actually quite good for an institution, notes Moffatt.

The guards in the boys' section were all male, with the exception of one female guard, who made herself popular with her charges by showing them card tricks. The guards for the most part were civil with the inmates, though "one of the older guards seemed to be make it his mission to get me to give up fighting to prove my innocence and just plead guilty. I suppose he felt I was guilty and wanted to see me punished for this horrible crime that I was charged with," says Moffatt.

On Sundays, religious groups came to offer services. Most residents found the services boring but attended anyway, because sometimes the proselytizers handed out free candies after the sessions were over.

Kids at the Juvenile Detention Centre stayed in all the time. The Centre wasn't equipped for outdoor activities, so the boys and girls were constantly indoors, regardless of the weather.

Moffatt spent much of his time at the place gearing up for his trial. So did police.

On October 17, 1956, Toronto Police sent Wayne Mallette's father, John Mallette, the following letter:

"Dear Sir: Ronald Moffatt who has been charged with Manslaughter in connection with the death of your son will be appearing in Toronto Juvenile Court, October 23, 1956, at 2:00 p.m.

On instructions from the Crown Attorney I enclose herewith two subpoenae for your attendance at the time, place and date referred to above. Your son Ronald is required owing to the fact that he was the last to have any contact with Wayne.

The Juvenile Court is located in the Registry Building, at Albert and Elizabeth Streets, ground floor. Toronto."

While the charge cited in the letter wasn't accurate, as it turned out, Moffatt's trial did begin that fall in Juvenile Court.

The presiding justice at Moffatt's trial was Juvenile Court Judge Lorne Stewart, whom Moffatt had faced earlier. Moffatt was being tried as a juvenile delinquent, not an adult, which meant there was no jury. Guilt or innocence would be solely decided by the judge.

Crown counsel at the trial was Henry Herbert Bull, while Moffatt's lawyer was Albert Knox (usually referred to as A.E. Knox by the press).

It would be a steep climb for Moffatt's defence team.

Born in 1911, Bull was a very competent Crown Attorney. According to the book, *Learned Friends*, a look at 50 prominent Ontario lawyers, Bull rehearsed his addresses to the jury in front of a mirror. He would study his reflected gestures and facial expressions, and ponder the tone of his voice. These theatrical deliberations complemented a thorough-going approach to the law.

"The man was meticulous in readying himself for the

courtroom. He left nothing to chance ... His clothes were immaculate, his posture ramrod straight, his manners impeccable. In all ways, he represented such a perfect embodiment of the Crown Attorney that the National Film Board, shooting a 1964 instructional movie about the workings of legal aid in York County, asked Bull to take the role of the prosecutor. No one else could play the part so convincingly. The NFB called it typecasting," noted *Learned Friends*.

Something else: in addition to being poised, smart and very well-prepared, Bull was also extremely tough.

"A brusque and intimidating man, Henry Herbert Bull lived up to his surname ... Bull was articulate and confident to the point of fearlessness and he didn't particularly care if he offended someone in or out of court. [By 1956] Bull had already been an assistant solicitor with the provincial treasury department, an assistant Crown Attorney, and a major in the Second World War," wrote author Robert J. Hoshowsky, in his book *The Last to Die*.

"Unwilling to lose in any situation, Henry Bull was passionate about the law; he was the archetype of what would become known as the Type A personality, which is associated with aggressive, impatient and competitive behavior as well as a greatly increased risk of hypertension and coronary heart disease," continued Hoshowsky.

Hoshowsky's book focused on Bull's prosecution of Arthur Lucas for two murders in Toronto in the early 1960s. Bull secured a conviction and Lucas was hanged December 11, 1962, in Toronto's Don Jail along with fellow murderer Ronald Turpin. The pair were the last two people hanged by the Canadian government. Capital punishment was already falling out of favour at the time, and would never be enforced again. In the mid-1970s, capital punishment was officially abolished in Canada.

That was the future, however. Back in the 1950s, the government was still happy to hang killers. In 1956, for example, four executions were carried out in Canada.

As a juvenile delinquent, Moffatt couldn't be hanged for killing Wayne Mallette. But he still faced the prospect of a long stretch in detention—a stretch marked by the odious distinction of having killed a child—an offence that rarely sits well with fellow convicts. Moffatt also feared that once he turned 18, he would be transferred to an adult facility and possibly hanged then.

Moffatt's defence team did have one formidable weapon on their side: a lengthy list of witnesses who placed Moffatt at the Metro Theatre at the time of Mallette's killing. Whether that would be enough to overcome Moffatt's confession remained unclear.

Chapter Four - The Trial

Months after her son's trial was over, Bette Moffatt would complain bitterly to reporters that "seven witnesses ... said he was at the theatre at the time the murder was committed" but that Judge Lorne Stewart didn't seem to care.

Mrs. Moffatt's math might not have been perfect, but she was correct in noting that several people testified that they saw her son at the Metro Theatre between 5:30 and 9:30 p.m.

Notes from Toronto Police files list the name, age and a thumbnail description of the testimony of these witnesses. An usher said he saw Moffatt at the Metro between 9:30 p.m. and 10:30 or 11 p.m. A theatre manager and an assistant manager both recalled seeing Moffatt at 9:30 p.m. A young boy attending the double feature saw Moffatt at 5:30 and 9:30 p.m., then from 11 to 11:30 p.m. The same boy was part of a group of kids, including Moffatt, who helped change signs on the theatre marquee after the movies ended. A 14-year-old claimed to have seen Moffatt around Bloor Street West (the street the Metro was located on) around 5 p.m.

There were also statements placing Moffatt at the

CNE grounds the day of Wayne Mallette's murder. Moffatt's old boss claimed he saw his ex-employee around the Rotor ride in the morning of September 15. The same person said Moffatt had also been at the CNE a few days earlier (at the time when Moffatt was in hiding). A CNE colleague told authorities Moffatt had been on the Exhibition grounds September 15. The same colleague said Moffatt was still hanging around there at 5:30 pm—when multiple other witnesses placed him at the Metro Theatre.

Moffatt today denies he was anywhere near the CNE the day Mallette died. He says he did his last shift at the Rotor on Labour Day and didn't make any subsequent visits in the days to follow.

The Crown had its own theory, largely based on Moffatt's confession to police. It was alleged that Moffatt did go to the Metro Theatre, but slipped out at some point, stole a bike, and cruised over to the deserted Exhibition grounds. There, he encountered Wayne Mallette and accidentally killed him. Moffatt fled the scene on his bicycle, bumped into a night watchman with whom he had a weird conversation, then biked away. Moffatt ditched his bicycle and walked to a restaurant near Bathurst and Queen Streets for a snack. Following a quick bite, he made his way back to the Metro to watch the rest of the show.

The confession didn't say if he walked, hitched a ride or took public transit to get from the restaurant to the Metro. According to Google Maps, it's roughly 2.5 kilometres from Bathurst and Queen Streets to 677

Bloor Street West. It would take about 30 minutes to walk, 16 minutes on the bus and eight minutes in a car to drive this distance.

Stomach content analysis pegged Wayne Mallette's time of death around 9 p.m.—when witnesses placed Moffatt at the movies. Stomach content analysis, then and now, is hardly an exact science, so the encounter between night watchman George Sinclair and the boy on the bike offers a better measure of the Crown's theory. In initial reports and media accounts, the encounter took place at 9 p.m. If the stomach content analysis was indeed correct, Sinclair met the teen cyclist a few minutes after Mallette was killed. Unless Moffatt was a speed eater who took a particularly fast cab, it's unlikely he could have met the night watchman at 9 p.m., walked to a restaurant for some food then made it to the Metro by 9:30 p.m.

Other reports suggested the encounter between Sinclair and the oddball youth happened shortly after he started his shift at 8:20 p.m. Moving the encounter back 40 minutes (and placing the murder earlier in the evening) would have given Moffatt more time to commit the crime, then carry out his subsequent actions. But that would suggest he was something of a sociopathic sadist, who could kill a child, eat a meal in a public restaurant, then go to a movie theatre to see his friends without showing any signs of panic or fear. Mallette's real killer—Peter Woodcock—was capable of such cold-blooded malice, but he wasn't the one on trial. Moffatt was hardly a straight arrow, but there's no indication he had deviant murderous impulses or steel nerves. Moffatt's performance in the courtroom should have given lie to any thoughts about him being cold-blooded. While the teenager tried his best to control his intense anxiety, he was frequently overwhelmed.

"The court room was an intimidating place. It reminded you of the old English-style court rooms where the judge is perched up high looking down on you," Moffatt states today.

Crown counsel Henry Herbert Bull prosecuted the case vigorously. Moffatt remembers the man as "very intimidating, though I realize that was part of his job to appear so."

Indeed, intimidation was all part of Bull's style: "When Henry Bull was in court everyone knew it—and few forgot him ... Judges, lawyers, jurors, police clerks, murders and thieves, remember the big, bushy eye brows and fierce blue eyes that flashed beneath," wrote the *Toronto Star*, on September 4, 1968.

While the *Star* described Bull as "a tough adversary", it noted he also had some whimsical traits, drawing cartoons and doodling during dull moments in court, and indulging in oil painting and watercolours at home.

Needless to say, Moffatt didn't get much opportunity to appreciate Bull's lighter side. Whenever the boy took the stand, Bull stood very close to him to issue questions. The teenager tried to remain composed but cried when the questioning got too harsh, or he grew frustrated when the Crown repeated the same questions again and again. Moffatt could take some comfort in the fact his mother and her sister, and even some old school friends came to the trial to offer moral support. He certainly needed it.

There was little direct physical evidence connecting Moffatt to the crime. In his confession, Moffatt claimed he stole a bicycle, rode it to the CNE then later ditched it. Needless to say, the bike was never found, despite an intense police search. A recovered bicycle with Moffatt's fingerprints on it would have been a devastating piece of evidence against him. As it stands, Moffatt says today he couldn't ride and the bike business—like the rest of his confession—was nonsense.

One of the few pieces of physical evidence the Crown did have centered on bite marks. Based on an examination of the bites on Mallette's body and impressions made from Moffatt's teeth, it was concluded Moffatt had indeed bitten the boy. Or so dental experts claimed. Other medical authorities had insights about the crime scene, Mallette's autopsy and the clothing and soil at the murder site—none of which in any conclusive way pointed to Moffatt's guilt.

DNA testing—which could have exonerated Moffatt and put police on Woodcock's trail—was still decades away. Such testing can provide almost 100 percent certainty in cases where viable evidence is available. Given that Mallette was ruthlessly bitten, the killer would have almost certainly left DNA traces on the poor boy's body. This could have been compared with Moffatt's DNA to confirm or absolve him as a suspect.

In the current court system, DNA is the gold standard of forensic evidence— "most people will consider it to be infallible," notes Osgoode Hall Law Professor Alan Young, in an interview.

Even without DNA, modern technology might have cleared Moffatt. Were Mallette murdered today, his killer's movements would likely be recorded on security cameras, on the street and at the CNE.

Police would later concede there was "very little corroborative evidence" to link Moffatt with Mallette's death, as the January 23, 1957 *Telegram* noted.

Nor were there any eyewitnesses who saw Moffatt commit the crime or even observe him together with little Wayne. And nobody noticed anything odd about Moffatt at the Metro Theatre the night of the murder (such as stains on his clothes, excessive sweat or extreme distress. The kind of signs that might be expected from a typical 14 year-old who just killed a child with his bare hands). As for Moffatt's subsequent behaviour, that was far less sinister than it seemed. Moffatt had gone into hiding after Mallette's death to avoid his father, not police. This fact had been widely reported in the press prior to the trial.

A *Telegram* story from September 22 said Moffatt was scared he'd be punished for skipping school. As a result, he "took extra bedclothes and food" and ran off, more or less. The *Star* offered similar details in a front page story that same day. When found by police in his hiding spot, Moffatt initially thought he was being picked up for cutting class.

None of this helped in the end. Moffatt's confession doomed his case. In the 1950s, it was difficult for people to grasp why anyone would confess to a crime they hadn't actually committed. Notions of police coercion or sloppy investigative work hadn't yet entered the popular consciousness.

Moffatt says his lawyer, Albert ("A.E.") Knox, "did a decent job of trying defend me" but that "the fix was in" and his guilt a forgone conclusion. Authorities were convinced they had the right suspect, in spite of Moffatt's solid alibi and testimony from multiple witnesses confirming that alibi.

The verdict soon was in: "Judge Stewart of juvenile court yesterday found a 14-year-old Toronto boy delinquent in the suffocation death of Wayne Mallette, 7, of Seeley's Bay," reported the *Globe* on December 5, 1956.

Moffatt was not sentenced, however. Juvenile Court Judge Lorne Stewart wanted Moffatt to have a psychiatric evaluation first.

"A program is being mapped out by court officials for the reformation of a 14-year-old schoolboy who was responsible for the suffocation death of Wayne Mallette, seven, last September. The boy will be returned to the Christie St. observation home where he was held awaiting trial until a complete social history is made of him by a team of psychiatrists and social workers. Now that the boy has been adjudged delinquent, the court must decide how he will be treated, a court official said,"

NATE HENDLEY

reported the *Toronto Daily Star* shortly after Moffatt's conviction.

This unnamed official was quoted as saying, "He will be dealt with not as an offender but one in a condition of delinquency. Therefore he will receive help and guidance and proper supervision. A program for his reformation will be established."

The *Star* outlined the options facing Moffatt once the psychiatric evaluation was completed: probation, foster care or an "industrial school" (that is, one of the so-called training schools the province operated at the time for juvenile delinquents).

Had he been tried and convicted as an adult, Moffatt could expect a more severe sentence. That did little to alleviate his fear of spending years in custody. When escorted from the courtroom, he felt suicidal and beyond despondent.

Moffatt spent his Christmas holidays at Toronto's Psychiatric Hospital. Located near the Ontario legislature (known as Queen's Park), the Hospital opened in 1925. By the mid-1950s, it was a place in transition.

"In keeping with then fashionable ideas of community psychiatry, the hospital had adopted a 'community living' approach to care, with the ward as a miniature community. Rather than the traditional custodial-inmate relationship of a mental hospital, TPH was stressing an informal, open-door policy. Mental illness was now regarded as a breakdown in living and treatment centered on readjusting people to society. These principles, also known as milieu therapy, represented all that was new and progressive in psychiatric care in the 1950s and 1960s. The essence of the therapy was providing a normal, healthy environment for the patients," stated the book, *TPH: History and Memories of the Toronto Psychiatric Hospital.*

At the same time, Toronto Psychiatric Hospital remained a foreboding place. Electroshock and insulin shock (in which non-diabetic patients were injected with the drug to induce a coma) were still part of the treatment regime for some patients. Psychosurgery was a burgeoning trend at the time, and lobotomies were occasionally performed on TPH patients.

Moffatt says his time at the Toronto Psychiatric Hospital actually wasn't that bad. He wasn't subjected to any medical torture and it was a respite from court, at least. Moffatt could look out at the Ontario legislature from a day sitting room.

"The male patient area was 'L' shaped with ... large dorms and a common area at one end. The shower and washroom area was located half way between the dorms and the private rooms and offices at the other end of the facility, which I found strange as when you were showering you were exposed to a steady stream of traffic going between the two wings of the 'L'," he recalls.

As a convicted prisoner, Moffatt was kept on a tight leash. He wasn't allowed to leave the specific area he had been assigned to and wander around. There were two other patients under equally tight security along with

Moffatt. One of the two had shot and killed his mother during a blackout but otherwise was a "very generous, pleasant guy" whom everyone liked, he recalls.

Meals at the hospital were decent and staff were "usually very pleasant and accommodating to the patients," continues Moffatt.

A large percentage of the psychiatric staff were female student nurses, doing mental health training. Attendants, who were male, kept watch to make sure no one became unruly. Should a patient get out of hand, attendants restrained them though typically they did so "with as little physical force as necessary," says Moffatt.

"Most of the patients there were not of the violent type, but most were there because of nervous break downs, etc. If a patient become unruly, after they had been subdued, they were usually sent to the Tubs (no this was not a form of medieval torture but a way of getting the patient relaxed). The patient was placed in a tub much like the one in your house's bathroom and placed in a canvas hammock. A canvas cover was placed over the patient to restrain them (there was an opening for the patient's head). Warm water was run over you, much like today's hot tub. You usually ended up going to sleep. It was quite pleasant and calming. A nurse was always in attendance to check on you," he states.

Moffatt says the head nurse was a middle-aged English lady who was usually cordial, though she could be stern if necessary.

Patient activities included dances, bingo and tennis.

Moffatt was unable to use the courts, however, because that would involve leaving his designated area.

Moffatt did experience drug therapy, but not in the form of insulin shock. He was injected with sodium pentothal, a so-called "truth serum" that puts patients in a dreamy, intoxicated state. The idea was that a patient would let their guard down and be more likely to reveal unpleasant truths under the influence of the drug. Moffatt was greatly annoyed when staff wouldn't tell him the results of his drugged experience.

Moffatt was in Toronto Psychiatric Hospital for roughly a month then returned to the Juvenile Detention Centre on Christie Street to await sentencing.

As Moffatt pondered what the judge had in store for him, his parents were desperately trying to hold things together. In a front-page interview with the *Star* published January 23, 1957, Bette Moffatt (identified merely as the "young mother" of the accused) talked about what her son's trial had done to her family.

"What can we do to prove his innocence? It has been a terrible experience for my husband and me. We have had to scrape and save to pay for his legal fees. We had to have our phone number unlisted and changed because cranks called us at all hours of the day and night to threaten us," she stated.

Moffatt's mother expressed hope that "a new development would come in the case" to prove her boy's innocence.

That development would come soon, but at terrible cost for another family.

On the afternoon of Saturday, January 19, 1957, Bernadette Voyce, who lived on Caithness Avenue north of Danforth Avenue in East Toronto, decided to pay a social call on neighbour and friend, Frieda Auld. Taking her four-year-old daughter Carole with her, Voyce walked three blocks to the Auld residence, at 1066 Danforth Avenue. Voyce went inside to have a cup of coffee with Mrs. Auld. Carole remained outside, playing with Auld's son Johnny, who was also four. Again, it is important to remember the social mores of the time. The era of helicopter parenting and hawk-like adult supervision was still in the future. In the mid-1950s, parents thought little of leaving even very young children outside, largely unsupervised. This attitude hadn't changed, despite the murders of Wayne Mallette and Gary Morris. The term "serial killer" hadn't been coined yet. The concept that someone was targeting and killing children was hard for Torontonians to comprehend, in spite of two recent deaths.

At some point, as Carole and Johnny played, a boy on a bicycle approached them. He seemed friendly enough, so the kids cheerfully bantered with him. The boy asked the kids how old they were. Both said "four". The stranger asked if they would like a ride on the handlebars of his nifty red racing bike. Both agreed. At first, the boy wanted to take Johnny. Then, he changed course and said he would take Carole first. He would come back and give Johnny a turn, he promised. Then the big kid cycled off, with Carole perched on his handlebars.

Johnny watched the pair head off towards Donlands Avenue. Then, according to the January 21 *Telegram*, he went inside his house and announced, "Mommy, Carole's gone for a ride on a bicycle with a high school boy."

Instantly alarmed, Voyce raced outside but couldn't see her daughter or the high school boy on the bicycle. A policeman named Constable Earl Newman happened to be making the rounds on Danforth Avenue. Voyce raced over and told him her daughter was missing. She told him what Johnny said about a high school boy on a bike. Constable Newman contacted the Pape Avenue police station and a cruiser soon arrived. Carole's increasingly anxious mother was given a ride around the neighbourhood by police, searching for her girl. At 4:20 p.m., a bulletin was released to all Metro Toronto police districts, notifying them about the case.

A major police search ensued. In the Don Valley, constables located a yardman with the city's parks department named Fred Callan who might have seen the suspect. Callan told police he saw a short, heavyset, dark-haired teenage boy pushing a bike on a set of rail tracks, heading north. The boy eventually reached a roadway, mounted his bike, and rode off.

Police flooded into the Don Valley, searching for the girl. Some 200 constables from stations in Toronto and East York joined in. Police dogs sniffed bushes and underbrush. Police from Toronto worked their way north while police from East York worked south. A separate contingent of peace officers searched Cherry Beach, on the hunch that whoever killed Gary Morris might have dumped Voyce there.

At 11 p.m., a dozen policemen, led by Detective-Sergeant Cecil Caskie started searching under the Prince Edward Viaduct. A concrete bridge spanning the Don Valley, the structure is commonly but incorrectly called the Bloor Viaduct. One of the men in the patrol, Constable Ernest Booth, located a body. It was a little girl, lying face-down in a puddle of congealed blood. The blue snowsuit she had been wearing had been removed. Her remaining clothes were torn and tangled.

"She was beaten, cut and kneed. She was mauled to death, an autopsy showed. The actual cause of death—a massive hemorrhage," stated the January 21 *Telegram*.

Constable Booth took out his service revolver and fired three shots in the air, a signal for other police to come quickly. He paused, then fired three more rounds. Dozens of officers soon arrived. Their ranks included Raymond Voyce, Carole's father. Police held him back from the crime scene, despite his desperate cries to see the body to determine if it was Carole.

It was her. Carole Voyce had become Peter Woodcock's third victim. The time of death was later estimated at sometime between 4 and 5 p.m. Police figured the suspect spent 30 minutes or more with his prey underneath the Prince Edward Viaduct. Given the volume of traffic overhead—traffic that would have included police cars searching for Voyce—this pointed to a very cold-blooded killer, unconcerned about being spotted.

On January 1, 1957, the City of Toronto police had merged with departments in surrounding areas to become the Metropolitan Toronto Police force. This widened jurisdiction experienced 15 "known" murders and three cases of manslaughter in 1957, according to the first annual Metropolitan Toronto Police report. Voyce was among the ranks of these victims.

Police took careful notes at the crime scene. There were two sets of footprints in the snow. Both sets led down a steep bank into the Don Valley. One set of footprints was larger than the other. The tracks led to the spot where Voyce was found. A single set of footprints led away from the murder site, to the north. There were also what appeared to be bike tire prints in the snow. These tracks ended at Mount Pleasant Road, around Roxborough Street East.

The description of the suspect, from Johnny Auld's account, was disturbingly familiar. Newspapers used this description to run huge "Wanted" style graphics on their front pages.

"Do You Know This Boy?" demanded a banner headline on the front page of the January 21 *Telegram*. Accompanying the headline was a big illustration of a teenage boy, with glasses and dark ruffled hair. The boy was standing next to a bicycle, which he gripped in his hands. The drawing was made by a *Telegram* sketch artist. The paper noted, not without a degree of pride, that the likeness had been "adopted as the official Metro

Toronto picture" of the suspect. As such, the illustration was distributed to all police stations in the Metropolitan Toronto area.

Just so people got the complete picture, the *Telegram* included a none-too-flattering written description of Voyce's suspected killer: "Features: Pimply face, dark hair combed back but parted. Wears horn-rimmed glasses. CLOTHING – He was wearing a dark brown windbreaker or short jacket, blue denim jeans and black shoes."

The police and press had finally realized they were likely dealing with a repeat offender. This was reflected in the intensity of the media coverage. While the murders of Mallette and Morris had been front-page news, Voyce's death generated an explosion of stories and speculation. The January 21, 1957 *Telegram*, for example, featured five pages of articles, photographs, drawings and maps about the murder. The following day, the *Toronto Daily Star* devoted almost three full pages to the story.

Reading the coverage today, it's possible to detect a whiff of hysteria, a sense that the murderer had to be caught fast. After Wayne Mallette was killed, police assured the public the killer had been found and jailed. Now two more kids had been killed, in equally horrible fashion. This sense of panic was reflected by headlines such as "Fear Boy to Kill Again" in the *Toronto Daily Star*.

Ironically, in covering Voyce's murder, the press underlined how easy it was for an innocent boy like Ron Moffatt to end up in custody. The issue of the *Telegram* with the drawing of the suspected killer also ran a story headlined, "All Boy Teeners Are Suspect."

"Every teenage boy who even roughly resembles the sadistic killer of four-year-old Carole Voyce is being swept into a 2,300 man police dragnet ... 'Get him before he kills again,' said Police Chief John Chisholm ... Personally aroused by a murder vicious beyond description, police intend to get him. If the search inconveniences a few hundred [teenagers], they feel it will be worth it," read the article.

The press made a direct connection between the killing of Voyce and Morris. "Coldly, methodically, the police are hunting throughout Metropolitan Toronto for a pimply-faced sex maniac who not only lured Carole from them in from of her home and killed her, but probably killed Gary Morris, nine, under similar circumstances four months ago," stated the January 21 *Telegram*.

In an interesting psychological tactic, authorities urged the mother of the murder suspect, whoever she may be, to turn her boy in. The basic idea, it seems, was that the murderer's mom might be guilt-tripped into helping police convict her son.

If Susan Maynard had any inclination that the pimply-faced sex maniac in question was her foster son, she didn't let on. Not too far into the future, Mrs. Maynard would speak extensively to reporters about Peter Woodcock's actions the day Voyce died. On that Saturday, Woodcock did some household chores, listened to music, had lunch then went to a store on Yonge Street, coming back around 1:30 p.m. After that, Woodcock took a ride on his bicycle.

It was all pretty standard behaviour on Woodcock's part. While cycling in winter might seem odd, it was something he did all the time so no one in the Maynard household thought anything of it. Mrs. Maynard said her foster son returned home for dinner after a few hours. While he had just murdered a four year old girl, Woodcock seemed perfectly at ease. After eating, the teenage killer read for a bit then headed off to his part-time job at Casa Loma, directing cars in the parking lot. Come Sunday, Woodcock was tired and didn't join the Maynard family for church. He opted instead to remain at home and watch television. He did not seem unnerved by all the attention police were giving to Voyce's death, much less the front page drawing that looked awfully like him.

While Woodcock remained at large, a reward was put together for information that might lead to the capture of Voyce's murderer. The Province of Ontario contributed $2,500 as did the Metro Police Commission, for a total of $5,000. Meanwhile, Deputy Chief Archie McCathie ordered a force of some 250 detectives to scour for clues. Police again looked around high schools, investigated bike racks and, interestingly enough, searched for truants. After all, "it was a report of a missing boy which solved the killing on the CNE grounds last September. Carole's death was the third child murder in Toronto in four months," noted the January 21 *Toronto Daily Star*.

Police were certain that whoever killed Voyce also

killed Morris, but still didn't connect the killings with Mallette. If authorities were way off base in this regard, they did zero in on a very important detail: Voyce's killer was likely someone who was familiar with the terrain in the Don Valley. Someone who knew the trails and topography of the place. It was an excellent hunch, and one that soon cracked the case.

Chapter Five - The Real Killer Caught

On Sunday evening, four young policemen prepared for the night shift at a police station in North York, a community that was part of Metropolitan Toronto. Constables George Douglas, John Small, Nevile Little and Bob McDonald began talking about the Carole Voyce case. One of the cops remembered something: didn't they handle a very similar case in the Don Valley the year before? That case also involved a young girl who had been reported kidnapped. Only it turned out she hadn't been kidnapped but was roaming around the Don Valley with a weird, slightly older boy. At the time, no one knew the boy in question planned to kill the girl. He only chickened out because it got dark and he worried about getting lost in the confusing Valley.

The four policemen called in their sergeant then leafed through occurrences from June 1956, which is when the previous incident occurred (other sources say March, but newspapers at the time said June). The cops also looked through their notebooks from that period. Eventually, someone found an entry about the weird kid. His name was Peter Woodcock and police also had his home address. From this moment on, Woodcock became the prime suspect in Voyce's murder.

The information gleaned by the four constables was turned over to Detectives Ted Blakely and James Crawford. The pair went to Woodcock's private school, Bloordale College, on Monday, January 21, 1957 and picked him up. By all accounts, Woodcock didn't resist when the law arrived.

Dets. Blakely and Crawford took Woodcock to a North York police station for questioning. Asked to account for his whereabouts on Saturday afternoon, Woodcock acknowledged he had been in the Don Valley. He claimed he saw a boy who just happened to look like him and happened to have a bike, racing away from the very location where Carole Voyce's body was found. Interestingly, it was virtually the same line that the mysterious teen on a bike told CNE watchman George Sinclair, the night Wayne Mallette was murdered.

Needless to say, police weren't buying it.

North York authorities turned Woodcock over to the City of Toronto cops. Around 2:30 p.m., Detectives Crawford and Blakely walked Woodcock through the doors of Toronto police headquarters at 149 College Street. The teenager was taken to an interrogation room. Woodcock looked "unworried" prior to questioning noted a *Toronto Daily Star* article published the next day.

Woodcock soon made a confession in which he admitting to killing Voyce. The confession didn't appear to be coerced in any way. Woodcock freely admitted his guilt. He was arrested for Voyce's murder, and charged that same day.

Around 6:40 p.m., accompanied by homicide squad detective George Sellar and other policemen, Woodcock was taken to east Toronto to retrace his movements with Voyce. "I want to make things straight," Woodcock allegedly told police, according to a *Globe and Mail* piece that following spring.

Police also went to the Maynard's Lytton Boulevard home to locate Woodcock's red and cream-coloured bicycle. Imprints were made of the tire tread to see if they matched bike tire marks found in snow and mud near Voyce.

In addition to being grilled about the Voyce murder, Woodcock was questioned about Gary Morris. Police would later take Woodcock down to Cherry Beach, to walk him through the Morris crime scene. Authorities also questioned Woodcock about other sexual and physical assaults on children that had taken place over the past couple of years. In many of these accounts, a young teenage boy on a bicycle approached children and molested them when the opportunity arose.

On January 22, Woodcock appeared in a police lineup viewed by Bill Christie, Morris' friend. After that, Woodcock was taken to court before Magistrate F.C. Gullen.

The confessed killer looked "like a typical teenage youth ... a clean-cut looking boy, Woodcock was short and of slight build, his black hair brush cut and hanging down in bangs. He was wearing horn-rimmed glasses and his face was slightly pimpled," noted a *Star* account published that same day.

"Are you Peter Maynard Woodcock?" asked Magistrate Gullen.

"Yes, your worship," stated Woodcock "in a clear, firm voice" wrote the *Star*.

The conversation between the two lasted less than a minute. The magistrate remanded Woodcock until January 29 and the boy was taken back to the cells where he was being held.

The press noted how scrawny Woodcock was, at five foot six inches tall and weighing a mere 100 pounds.

At first, Woodcock's legal defence was taken up by lawyer Robert Montgomery and Billy Maynard, Woodcock's older step-brother. A fourth-year law student, Billy worked in Montgomery's law office. The pair complained they had not been allowed to talk with Woodcock the day he was arrested. By doing so, police denied Woodcock the benefit of legal counsel. If nothing else, Toronto police were being consistent. They had interrogated Ron Moffatt without a lawyer present as well. In Moffatt's case, however, authorities waited five hours before informing his parents their son was in custody for allegedly murdering a child. The Maynards, by contrast, were informed shortly after Woodcock was taken for questioning then charged with murder.

The Maynards reaction to Woodcock's arrest was

played out all over the media. A front page *Star* story published January 22 bore the headline, "Foster Family is Stunned, Gave Peter Everything".

"He has been such a wonderful boy ... just like our own son. I won't believe it until I talk to Peter myself," Mrs. Maynard told the *Star*.

Billy Maynard seemed equally supportive, stating, "We will certainly defend him. I've been a big brother to him for many years. We were his family and a happy one, too. Peter came to us from the Children's Aid Society when he was just a little tot. Mother wanted to do things to help out in the war effort and she took several homeless waifs. Peter was the favourite and we accepted him as one of the family."

The Maynard mother and son ticked off Woodcock's good qualities: he liked trains and streetcars and had an encyclopedic knowledge of the city's transit system. He enjoyed operas and ballet scores over Elvis and rock 'n roll in general. He was a good conversationalist, was neat and tidy, sang in the church choir, did well in school and didn't smoke. Susan Maynard wasn't above a little fudging of the truth, telling the *Star* that Woodcock had "a few friends" when all evidence indicated he didn't have any.

Mrs. Maynard said her husband, Frank, was so horrified by the news he had taken ill and was in bed.

Further newspaper accounts detailed Woodcock's sad past. It was noted that Woodcock had been abandoned by his birth mother and became a ward of Children's

Aid. The media also cited his extensive medical history. Stories in the press also noted how the Maynards stood by their boy, and tried to get him help for his medical and later mental problems, as they emerged.

Things began moving quickly. Two days after Woodcock's arrest, Robert Montgomery quit the case, saying he would no longer represent the boy as his counsel. Newspaper accounts did not say why. Woodcock, who was still a ward of the Children's Aid Society, as the Maynards never formally adopted him, would be defended by lawyers from that group.

Shocking as Woodcock's arrest was for the city and his foster family, it brought a glimmer of hope to Ron Moffatt. Now that Woodcock had been arrested, maybe authorities would realize they'd charged the wrong boy in Wayne Mallette's death.

The press picked up on the changing tempo in the Mallette murder case.

"CNE Case Reopened May Free Boy – Murder Confession False?" read a front-page headline in the *Telegram* on January 23. Authorities, said the article, were pondering "new information" in the Mallette murder. "If this boy didn't do it, then he will be freed," stated Deputy Police Chief Archie McCathie, referring to Moffatt.

A *Star* piece that same day offered further details. Police had reopened the Mallette case and "a full-scale new investigation" was underway. "Disclosures by Woodcock are reported to clear the Vanauley St. boy," wrote legendary police reporter Jocko "Gwyn" Thomas in the *Star*.

Among the details that police were pondering was the fact that Gary Morris, like Wayne Mallette, had been savagely bitten. A medical report based on a mould of Moffatt's teeth entered at his trial seemed to point to him as the person who bit Mallette. However, now it looked like that evidence might have been wrong. Certainly, it seemed more than coincidental that two young murder victims had been bitten in the same manner. This would seem to indicate the same killer had attacked both kids.

Police were also looking into non-fatal attacks on other children in the Toronto-area that closely matched the assaults on Mallette, Morris and Voyce. The media reported there might have been a dozen such recent cases. Some of these attacks might easily have resulted in additional deaths. The January 23 *Telegram* reported on the case of an eight-year-old girl who took a ride on "a youth's bicycle near her Etobicoke home" on December 31 of the previous year. The girl was subsequently choked and stripped and left naked underneath the Queen Elizabeth Way viaduct. If the girl hadn't regained consciousness she could have frozen to death. The case was not initially made public because the family involved didn't want to subject their daughter to the ensuing publicity. Another young girl was allegedly taken to "a deserted playground in Forest Hill by a bike riding youth," reported the *Telegram*, referring to an upscale Toronto neighbourhood. The boy started strangling the girl, only to abandon her and ride off when a car approached.

The press also noted that Moffatt himself stoutly defended his innocence (in spite of his supposed confession to police). It was stated the boy had requested a lie detector test to clear him. This had been denied, but the newspapers did mention that Moffatt had undergone a sodium pentothal test at Toronto Psychiatric Hospital, the results of which still had not been revealed.

According to the *Star*, the Attorney-General's office, the Crown Attorney's office and Judge Lorne Stewart had been briefed on the situation by police.

"Some details of the convicted boy's statement to police last fall were proved to be incorrect and were attributed to 'imagination' at his juvenile court hearing. However, he was convicted by Judge Lorne Stewart," wrote the *Star*.

As a result of all these new revelations, W.B. Common, Director of Prosecutions, announced that leave to appeal Moffatt's conviction had been granted "on points of law," continued the *Star*. Translated, this meant an appeal could go forward.

The news was a huge relief to the Moffatt family.

"My boy is innocent and my prayers have been answered that a new development would come in the case," said Bette Moffatt (who went unnamed) in the January 23 *Telegram*.

Mrs. Moffatt said doctors hadn't released the results of Ron's sodium pentothal test because it clearly showed he was innocent. Authorities, she said, didn't want to admit their mistake. She also spoke wearily about how legal costs were exhausting the family's resources.

The same day the *Telegram* story ran, Deputy Chief McCathie promised to put together a full report on whatever new investigation was being made in the Mallette case. The Attorney-General would get a copy, insisted the deputy chief.

If the Moffatt family were jubilant, Mallette's real killer was, by all accounts, calm and collected now that he was in police custody. Psychiatrists were preparing to probe Woodcock's mind to see how a teenager—even a severely maladjusted one—could commit such horrible crimes.

As shrinks sized up Peter Woodcock, the wheels of justice continued to turn—slowly.

On January 24, Justice Eric Gelling Moorhouse of the Ontario Supreme Court adjourned a hearing into an application for leave to appeal Moffatt's arrest. The adjournment was for one month.

Despite being convicted for juvenile delinquency in the death of Wayne Mallette, Moffatt still hadn't been sentenced. Justice Stewart had been putting this task off until he received a full report from the doctors examining Moffatt at the Toronto Psychiatric Hospital. Being thoroughly scrutinized by doctors and mental health specialists would be about the only thing Moffatt and Woodcock would ever have in common.

February 1 marked the day of Moffatt's sentencing.

Despite the new information about his case and Woodcock's arrest, Moffatt was committed to the Ontario Training School for Boys based in Bowmanville, Ontario. It wasn't an adult jail, but a facility for juvenile offenders. Small comfort, for a very scared convicted killer.

Woodcock's arrest had been one bright spot in the darkness surrounding Ron Moffatt.

Another development occurred around the same time that would have an equally significant impact. Moffatt had a new lawyer. His name was Ernest Patrick Hartt. Patrick Hartt, as he was generally known, would prove to be a formidable ally in the fight to clear the boy's name.

Hartt worked for renowned criminal defence lawyer Goldwin Arthur Martin, whose office was located at 320 Bay Street in downtown Toronto. Martin was somewhat of a pioneer in his field. After graduating first in his class at Osgoode Hall Law School in 1938, Martin's peers were astonished he chose to become a criminal lawyer, defending people accused of breaking the law.

"At the time, criminal lawyers were widely regarded as a lower form of the profession. But early in Martin's practice, he found a moral base to his choice ... He set an example in advocacy that brought new respectability to criminal work," stated the book, *Learned Friends*.

There are file folders bulging with letters to both Martin and Hartt from grateful clients in the Archives of the Law Society of Upper Canada (LSUC) at Osgoode Hall. Many of these letters are written on prison stationery. Inmates praise the men for their work in court and help in getting them released or their cases appealed.

Hartt was a serious, precocious child of high intellectual caliber and empathic spirit who grew up in London, Ontario. He studied at Osgoode Hall Law School in Toronto, graduating in 1953. He did not lose his empathy for the underdog: as a lawyer Hartt "found it painful to visit clients in prison because of the inequality of their situations," wrote June Callwood in a profile published November 17, 1975 in the *Globe and Mail*.

Despite, or maybe because of, his concern for social justice, Hartt would have a spectacular legal career, serving as a judge in a series of high profile positions. In the early 1970s, he chaired the Law Reform Commission of Canada and frequently made the front pages of major newspapers.

Oddly enough, Hartt's boss was close friends with Crown Attorney Henry Bull. Martin and Bull had been classmates and were long-time pals.

Friendship was one thing; however, a court battle was another. A battle that Martin's law firm—spearheaded by Hartt—took on with gusto and skill.

The page for Thursday, January 24, 1957 in Martin's office day planner contains a note about a speech at the Empire Club. This is followed by the single word

"Moffat" written in pencil. The misspelled Moffatt family name appears again, on Thursday, February 21 in the same office planner, stored in the LSUC Archives.

As the notations indicate, Hartt was on the case.

It had been Hartt who obtained leave to appeal Moffatt's conviction. Hartt's task had not been made easier by the fact the 30-day time limit for issuing an appeal had passed by the time he got involved. No matter. Hartt forged on, hammering away at the legitimacy of Moffatt's confession to police. In the end, the appeal period was extended. The man who granted the extension was Chief Justice James McRuer, who would later make an equally important ruling in Moffatt's case.

Getting the appeal rolling was just the first of Hartt's acts in securing Moffatt some justice. He would prove a dogged defender of Moffatt, just when the terrified boy needed all the support he could get.

Chapter Six - In and Out of Custody

On February 1, 1957, Ron Moffatt was placed in the Ontario Training School for Boys in Bowmanville, Ontario. The Training School housed male offenders who weren't quite adults but weren't children either. As its name implied, the facility emphasized rehabilitation and education, at least in theory.

Moffatt for one, was not impressed.

"I hated it there and from the moment I arrived I wanted out. The inmates were housed in cottages, roughly 20 to 30 boys per unit. The older boys were sort of in charge and if they didn't like you they could make it rough for you ... I just couldn't accept the fact that I could be spending the rest of my life in places like this," he explains today.

While the press reported Moffatt might be freed after turning 18, he feared this wasn't true. Some authorities warned him that he would be transferred to adult prison after reaching his 18th birthday. There, Moffatt would find himself among hardened cons who hated child killers. Moffatt also faced the lingering worry he might be hanged.

The facility Moffatt found himself in had been launched with great fanfare in August, 1925. It was the first of what would become roughly a dozen training schools the province operated across Ontario for juveniles.

"The school, which strived to distance itself from anything suggestive of an institution, was situated on 300 acres [121 hectares] of picturesque land on the northeast outskirts of Bowmanville, a town 50 miles [80 km] east of Toronto. Farm work came to form the nucleus of the school, which eventually grew to involve five residential dormitories, a full technical workshop, swimming pool and gymnasium, and large dining and administrative buildings," stated a 1988 book called *Bowmanville Training School Through the Years*.

In the 1940s, the Training School housed German prisoners of war. When World War Two ended, the prisoners were transferred, and the facility became a custodial centre for juvenile delinquents again.

A total of 543 boys were "under supervision" at different times at Bowmanville during the fiscal year ending March 31, 1957, according to an Ontario government report. These students hadn't necessarily broken any laws. At the time, Ontario family court judges could commit young people to training schools simply for being unruly, disobedient or "incorrigible". Sometimes judges packed kids off at the behest of parents or guardians who found their offspring had become unmanageable.

Upon arrival at Bowmanville, inmates were steered into a Reception Unit. There, a committee determined the most appropriate "class, shop, house, group, supervisor, etc.," for the boy. Doctors, psychologists and other officials all weighed in, stated a 1959 report on Ontario training schools.

"The new boy is shown vocational classes, receives information on his duties and responsibilities, is given a preview of the rules of the school and how soon he can expect placement. There is an appeal to the intelligence of the boy, which is commendable," explained the report.

In a summary of his own, covering the April 1, 1956 – March 31, 1957 fiscal year, Bowmanville superintendent John Morrison elaborated on the school's mission.

"Training is developed on a four-point basis: Academic, Vocational, Programme and After-Care. Academic studies are directed toward maintaining and expanding school grades. The curriculum as laid down by the Department of Education is followed ... Our Vocational Shops provide trades' training for the boys. Most of our students spend a half-a-day in shop and half-day in academic classes," wrote Morrison.

The Training School had a machine shop, greenhouse, paint shop, auto shop and laundry room and courses in subjects such as woodworking, sheet metal, shoe repair and horticulture.

For extracurricular fun or physical training, boys

could indulge in "soccer, ice hockey, basketball, floor hockey, volleyball, badminton, lacrosse, baseball and swimming. Our uniformed forty-piece bugle band played for twenty-three organizations during the summer and fall months," added Morrison.

There was also daily religious instruction involving morning prayers, hymns and scripture—a facet of trainingschool life that got Moffatt into deep trouble. Moffatt wasn't sure if his fellow delinquents knew what he had been convicted of, but he didn't like most of them anyway. When one of the few kids he did get along with approached him with a view to breaking out, he was all ears. The plan centered on the religious instruction that was supposed to steer wayward boys to righteousness.

"On Sundays you had to go to Sunday School and usually the guard that took you there was an older gentleman, so we figured while we were in the midst of our journey to church we would just run away, and this old fellow would never be able to chase us. This was the GREAT PLAN. Meanwhile this all happened in the middle of winter and the ground was covered with snow and to our great surprise the guards don't chase after you, inmate trustees do. Needless to say, we didn't get far," recalls Moffatt.

The consequences were brutal. Moffatt was taken back to his cottage and forcibly stripped along with his accomplice, and paraded naked before his peers. The morning following his failed escape, Moffatt found himself forced to stand, barefoot, in his underwear, on cold terrazzo-flooring in a tiny detention room. He had

NATE HENDLEY

to remain standing on this freezing slab most of the day. Moffatt was not permitted to lean against the wall for support. At night, he slept on the same floor, with one woolen blanket. When he wasn't standing or sleeping, Moffatt had to get on his hands and knees and clean the floor with a small scrub brush. To make matters worse, Bowmanville practised the old military tradition of collective punishment. All the inmates in Moffatt's cottage lost their privileges, as a result of his escape attempt. Needless to say, this didn't endear Moffatt to his peers.

Moffatt also attracted the ire of a particular, red-haired guard who took to smacking him on the back of the head and cursing him out in front of the other boys.

To get away from such misery, Moffatt came up with another bad plan.

"All I could think about was: 'How in the hell am I going to get myself out of this?' So I finally came up with the idea of playing crazy and pretending I was losing it. They finally sent me to see the resident shrink and he told them I should be sent for a psychiatric evaluation. So I was on my way out of Bowmanville and to my horror [placed in] Guelph Reformatory's psychiatric wing. I figured I was going back to the Toronto Psychiatric Hospital," he states.

In total, Moffatt spent less than a month at the Ontario Training School for Boys in Bowmanville, before being transferred to the psychiatric unit at the Ontario Reformatory, Guelph.

Also called the Guelph Reformatory, the Ontario Reformatory, Guelph, had been built in the 1910s in a rural locale. The original buildings were designed in neo-classical style, to obscure the fact they were part of a prison complex. Someone who wasn't paying close attention might mistake the buildings for a college, at first. The design was a reflection of the intent to rehabilitate prisoners, through farm-work and other various programs intended to make them productive citizens.

These reformist sentiments were severely tested on July 5, 1952, when a riot broke out at the facility. It only lasted a few hours, but prisoners significantly damaged the prison interior. A later investigation couldn't turn up any specific causes of the riot, other than that some prisoners were antisocial and that security wasn't as good as it could be. As a result, security measures were enhanced, and some dormitory windows bricked up or covered with grilles.

Still, the Ontario Reformatory, Guelph, retained a touch of its rustic ambiance, at least on the lead-up to the prison complex itself.

An article in *The Globe Magazine*, from February 19, 1966, offered a good description of what the place was like on first arrival:

"It was almost noon when the bus turned off No. 21 Highway into the reformatory grounds. It didn't look much like a prison. No high stone walls. No turrets. Just waist-high stone fences—obviously the work of inmates—and hundreds of acres of rolling farmland.

The complex of grey buildings that came into view, a minute later looked more like a school than a jail ... The illusion was lost inside. Ten minutes later they were all sitting in the green admitting room in the basement of the main building. Now it looked like a prison. Barred windows. Grilled doors with heavy locks. The antiseptic glare of scrubbed floors. The handcuffs Jimmy shared with the young arsonist ... were removed and three khaki-uniformed custodial officers were barking orders—'Sit quietly! You can smoke but keep quiet!'"

As the article implied, for all its rolling farmland, the Ontario Reformatory, Guelph, remained a place of fear and dread. Certainly, that's how Moffatt felt when he entered his new home.

"When I arrived at the Guelph Reformatory, my memory went back to watching old prison movies and how the new arrivals felt as the big steel doors slammed behind them and they entered the bowels of the beast. I was terrified. I was told to shower, then given my clothing. I was taken up to the hospital wing and led to a separate room where I spent that first night. It was late by the time we arrived at the institution and by the time I had been processed, it was time for 'Lights Out'. Next morning one the inmates came in and introduced himself to me and reassured me that nobody would harm me (he was one the toughest guys in the prison, as I found later) and he said, 'If I should need anything, or wanted to know anything, just ask.' I already felt a little safer," recalls Moffatt.

In the 1950s, the Guelph Reformatory typically

housed between 1,500 – 1,700 men and boys at any time. This was a provincial facility which meant no one stayed there for long. Prisoners were serving sentences "ranging from three months to a theoretical maximum of four years less two days," read the 1967 book, *Society Behind Bars – A Sociological Scrutiny of Guelph Reformatory.* Anyone sentenced to a longer stretch would have served their time in a federal institution.

The Ontario Reformatory, Guelph, boasted an abattoir, a plant making automobile licence plates, a cannery, machine and tinsmith shop, tailor shop, carpentry department, and a woollen mill making blankets and socks. Crops were planted in the farmland and a dairy herd kept on the property. There was also a hospital, psychiatric clinic, dining halls, classrooms, library, gym and outdoor playing facilities.

Prison employees were assigned military ranks and khaki-style military uniforms. They were expected to conduct themselves in precise, disciplined military style. At the time Moffatt was there, the staff consisted of one superintendent, three assistant superintendents, one captain, eight lieutenants, nine sergeants, 13 corporals and 230 guards, plus support and administrative personnel.

Society Behind Bars examined what the prison was like in the early 1960s, a few years after Moffatt served time there.

"It is no secret in Ontario that for many years the Guelph Reformatory has been the butt of criticisms by various informed persons and even groups, all of whom have alluded to its crime-teaching functions. These functions are, of course, by-products of the existence of an inmate sub-culture centered on antisocial values," stated the book.

As with most prisons, there was a hierarchy of crime at Guelph. Sex offenders and anyone causing harm to children ranked near the bottom of the hierarchy. Just as he had been in Bowmanville, Moffatt was terrified his status as a convicted child-killer put him at risk.

"My worst fears were that the other inmates would find out what I had been charged with. Even though I was innocent, I had been found guilty and many believed at that time before new evidence came forward, that I was guilty. Anybody going into a prison system with charges that relate to harming children is a 'cooked goose'. There are no secrets in prison. The 'Rumour Mill' makes certain of that. A guard tells an inmate and then it is all over the system. So I was certain they knew what I was there for, but it was quite some time before I was ever questioned about it by other inmates and to my surprise, most of them seemed satisfied that I was innocent," he recalls.

Moffatt found himself assigned to floor cleaning duties in the hospital building. He had to wax the floors, a job considerably more strenuous than it sounds. For this task, Moffatt couldn't rely on a new buffing machine but "an old fashioned apparatus that consisted of a 50 pound weight attached to a long handle that you put rags under and pushed back and forth down a 12 foot wide x 150 foot long hallway. It was quite a work out," he states.

Formal exercise consisted of visits to the gym two or three times a week. During warm weather months, inmates played baseball outside. When it was cold, they played ice hockey. Other athletic diversions included basketball, soccer, touch rugby, horseshoe pitching, etc. Moffatt recalls a heavy punching bag was set up "for guys to take their frustrations out on instead of on another inmate."

"In all prisons there is a certain amount of homosexuality. I was never involved in any sexual activity, but I was what they called a 'KID'. This is comparable to having a boyfriend. They look out for you and get you things you need. I had one guy who first introduced himself to me at Guelph, he never tried to approach me for sex but let everybody know I was 'off limits'. This guy, even though he was one of the toughest ones in the prison, seemed like a good guy, and very compassionate. I truly believed he thought I got a raw deal and felt sorry for me. As more evidence about my case came to light, many others including the guards would come to feel the same way," continues Moffatt.

That evidence was slowly coming to light on the outside. On March 1, the hearing into Moffatt's appeal was adjourned by Justice Percy Smily of the Ontario Supreme Court. A law student named James Jerome, who was working for Patrick Hartt, requested the adjournment because Hartt had chickenpox.

By April, Hartt had sufficiently recovered to visit Peter

Woodcock in prison, along with Woodcock's lawyer, John Brooke and a police officer. All three men "wanted to be sure that Woodcock would testify to his guilt" in the murder of Wayne Mallette, wrote Mark Bourrie in *By Reason of Insanity*.

Woodcock had not been charged with killing Mallette—or Gary Morris for that matter. He was being tried solely with the murder of Carole Voyce. As Woodcock was slightly older than Moffatt, he was being tried as an adult in front of a jury. If convicted, he could be hanged. Hartt wanted to find out if the alleged child-murderer could cast some light on Mallette's death and help free Ron Moffatt.

Woodcock's trial began April 8 before Justice Wishart Flett Spence of the Ontario Supreme Court in Toronto. In a sign of the times, the front page of the *Toronto Daily Star* that day contained articles about both the Woodcock trial and the plight of eight girls expelled from a convent school in Ottawa for attending a rock 'n roll concert featuring Elvis Presley.

In court, Elvis-hating Woodcock took the stand and pled not guilty "in a firm, clear voice," wrote the *Star*.

Like Moffatt, Woodcock took a not-guilty plea despite having admitted his crimes to police. The difference being, Woodcock confessed voluntarily and was truly guilty.

On April 9, Woodcock's confession, made earlier that year, was read out loud by Assistant Crown Attorney Arthur Klein. In it, Woodcock admitting to killing Voyce and sexually assaulting roughly a dozen other boys and girls. Woodcock looked "pale" while the confession was read but otherwise "listened with no show of emotion," reported the *Toronto Daily Star*.

In his initial address to the jury, John Brooke didn't deny the veracity of the confession but said his client had severe psychiatric problems.

"You will probably have gathered that the defence of Peter Woodcock will be that he is insane in the extent that he should be excused of all responsibility for criminal acts ... Our law doesn't punish a man or hang him because he is insane. He is detained by the government until they see fit to release him ... The result of a decision by you that this boy is insane is that he would be incarcerated forthwith," wrote the *Globe* on April 11.

Crown Prosecutor Klein called some 50 witnesses during the trial while Brooke, called six. Four of the six defence witnesses were psychiatrists who told the court Woodcock was mentally ill. It was noted that Woodcock was a social pariah among his peers who brutally picked on him and was probably schizophrenic. Were the latter true, Woodcock might not have been aware that torturing and killing Voyce was wrong, said experts.

Susan Maynard testified that her foster son was "a social misfit, a poor lonely child who longed for friends but never had one all his life ... He was beaten up by other children all his life," stated the *Globe*.

On the stand, Maynard was asked about Woodcock's

actions on the afternoon of Saturday, January 19. This was the day the teenager took a bike ride, abducted Carole Voyce then murdered her in the Don Valley. According to his foster mom, Woodcock "came home a normal, sweet child, his hands and face clean, his clothes spotless," that evening, noted the *Globe*. Maynard also said she had no idea her foster child was molesting kids around the city and still refused to believe such accusations.

There was no disagreement, however, that Woodcock was seriously disturbed. The judge, Crown and defence all agreed on that point. This was not just opinion, but an issue of law.

On April 11, the jury returned their verdict at 2:31 p.m., following a two-hour deliberation that included a lunch break. Woodcock, they decided, was not guilty by reason of insanity.

Woodcock "did not flinch at the verdict" and remained "as impassive as he had throughout the trial," reported the April 12 *Globe and Mail*.

The verdict did not mean Woodcock was free. Under the rules of the day, Woodcock could still be held in a psychiatric facility, which is exactly what the court had in mind.

Justice Spence ordered the boy to stand, which he did.

"Peter Woodcock, you have heard the verdict of the jury. Therefore I order you kept in strict custody in the Toronto Psychiatric Hospital until the pleasure of the Lieutenant-Governor is known," pronounced the judge.

Woodcock would remain institutionalized until authorities saw fit to release him, presumably after he was cured. Should Woodcock show no signs of improvement or rehabilitation, he could remain hospitalized for life, despite his not-guilty verdict.

"After the judge ordered Woodcock to be removed, the youth stepped from the prisoner's box and marched from the courtroom between two sheriff's officers. He walked with a bouncy step and his arms swung slightly," noted the *Globe*.

Two days after the verdict, the *Globe* offered a poignant editorial.

"The tragic story of Peter Woodcock has come to an unhappy conclusion and the boy will be subject to confinement in an appropriate institution, probably for the rest of his life," wrote the newspaper.

As Woodcock contemplated lifelong institutionalization, Moffatt's future was also being decided by a judge with a reputation for toughness. The judge was James McRuer, the same justice who had granted an extension on Hartt's leave of appeal a few months back. Despite this ruling, McRuer was no softy; in fact, his judicial nickname was "Hangin' Jim". McRuer acquired this sobriquet for his propensity to send defendants to the gallows. Among other rulings, McRuer sentenced Steve Suchan and Lennie Jackson of the Boyd Gang to hang for killing a cop.

"To this day, some consider McRuer Canada's greatest

law reformer, while others say he was the nastiest person they ever met," stated the book *The Last to Die.*

As things turned out, Moffatt would be more likely to agree with the first part of that assessment.

Chief Justice McRuer's ruling on Hartt's appeal, issued April 16, was dense with legalese. It noted that Moffatt had been convicted "by His Honour Judge Stewart, Juvenile Court Judge for the County of York on the 4th day of December, 1956" for killing "one, Wayne Mallette, age seven years."

The document further observed that Moffatt had been initially placed in the Bowmanville Training School and was "now a prisoner at the Ontario Reformatory in Guelph."

While the language in most of the ruling was clotted, the judge's concluding remarks were clear: "Upon hearing Counsel for the said Ronald Moffatt and for the Attorney General for the Province of Ontario ... it is further ordered that the said conviction [against Moffatt] is hereby squashed and a new trial is hereby directed."

The teenager from Vanauley Street would have a second chance to prove his innocence.

Chapter Seven - Retrial

Justice James McRuer's ruling set the wheels in motion for a retrial. Immediately after the judge issued his order, Patrick Hartt applied for a judicial order to have Peter Woodcock released to testify at the retrial. Woodcock had been placed in a mental hospital in Penetanguishene, Ontario on April 20, 1957.

Hartt's application was successful. On May 3, Judge Percy Smily issued a writ of habeus corpus, which meant that Woodcock could be transported to Toronto to testify. Hartt wanted Woodcock to tell a courtroom what really happened to Wayne Mallette, and clear his client in the process.

Back in the psychiatric unit at the Guelph Reformatory, Moffatt was delighted with how events were unfolding.

"When it was found out that I had won my appeal, everyone was cheering me on, so my stay at Guelph was quite pleasant under the circumstances. All of sudden, out of the blue, two detectives showed up at Guelph to escort me back to Toronto ... I didn't realize how close I was to my freedom," recalls Moffatt.

Freedom came in the form of an order from Judge Lorne Stewart, of the Juvenile and Family Court of the

Municipality of Metropolitan Toronto. Dated Tuesday, May 7, 1957, the note ordered the superintendent of the Guelph Reformatory to release Moffatt into police custody, to be transported to Juvenile Court in Toronto. Ironically, Judge Stewart had presided over Moffatt's first trial and pronounced him guilty.

Three days later, another note, from the superintendent of the Ontario Reformatory, Guelph, listed Moffatt's personal effects, which amounted to a watch, ring and other trinkets. It was documented that the prisoner had no cash on him. The note was signed by an escorting police officer.

Moffatt's new trial commenced May 13 in Juvenile Court on Jarvis Street before Judge Harold Fuller. When Moffatt wasn't in the courtroom, he was held at the Juvenile Detention Centre on Christie Street.

Once again, there was no jury because the defendant was being tried as a juvenile, not an adult. Reporters were not allowed to report on day-to-day proceedings. They would, however, be allowed to report on the outcome of the trial when the verdict came in and offer other details about the case.

"Judge Harold Fuller, who is both a county judge and juvenile court judge in Welland was brought in following a special order in council to hear the second trial," explained the May 17 *Toronto Daily Star*.

Moffatt was represented in court by Hartt and lawyer Albert ("A.E.") Knox, from his first trial. For a return engagement, the Crown counsel was the aggressive Henry Herbert Bull.

As expected, Woodcock was the star witness at Moffatt's second trial. Hartt told reporters that Woodcock could provide "very relevant evidence," wrote the May 14, *Globe and Mail*. That he did, though Moffatt was less than impressed with the convicted killer.

Woodcock "looked like a Sunday school kid. Kind of a runt ... When I first saw him he looked like this big sad little kid. He had glasses. He looked like he'd sit in the back of the class and be picked on all the time," states Moffatt.

While Woodcock had indeed been terribly victimized as a child, Moffatt sensed some very disturbing vibes coming from the teenager. Behind his glasses, Woodcock had "dead eyes" Moffatt recalls. On the stand, Woodcock was equally chilling, as he calmly confessed to Wayne Mallette's murder, he adds.

Awful as it might have been, Woodcock's testimony went a long way in vindicating Moffatt. The Vanauley Street boy also benefitted from the legal firepower provided by Patrick Hartt.

While Moffatt admits he "never had much faith" in Knox, his view of Hartt is considerably more favourable

"I felt really confident when I saw him up there, questioning witnesses ... he was pit bull tenacious," recalls Moffatt.

If he was delighted by Hartt's performance, Moffatt was somewhat bewildered by the medical evidence at the second trial. When Moffatt first went on trial, dental evidence was entered in court that supposedly indicated he had bitten Mallette. Now, it was stated that the bites on Mallette's body were not in fact inflicted by Moffatt. This sudden change of opinion has never been explained. Moffatt has his own theories, but the most likely explanation is simply bad science. Criminal forensics at the time was crude, to put it mildly.

Dental evidence aside, one of the biggest differences between Moffatt's first and second trial was the mindset of the defendant. Moffatt had spent much of the first trial in abject terror, sometimes breaking down in tears on the witness stand in the face of brutal questioning. He was considerably more poised and confident the second time around. Again, he faced harsh questions on the stand, but this time was better prepared and sharper with his answers.

"Bull was the Crown Attorney during my second trial and as usual he was right in my face. However, I stood toe-to-toe with him this time and even screamed at him about how the police intimidated me and had a 14-year-old boy terrified during the interrogation," Moffatt recalls today, with a touch of pride at his youthful defiance.

It was all over in a matter of days.

On May 16, Justice Fuller issued his verdict. He opened with a sharp criticism of police procedure:

"There is one other observation and that is to do with certain statements taken by the police. In my County,

I have suggested to the police that in all cases where statements are being taken from juveniles, there should be present either the parents, or one of the parents, or some other disinterested person such as a minister, priest [or] teacher; or if they are not available, at least some other person not connected with the police, and I would suggest that that practice is advisable and if it were followed it would be unlikely to have a situation arise such as did arise in this particular case."

Justice Fuller moved on to discuss Peter Woodcock's testimony:

"This case has been an unusual one in that, for one thing, there was presented to the court two convictions, each of which contain considerable detail as to how this offence was committed. In the case of Peter Woodcock, he was a person to be declared to be of unsound mind, but in the evidence presented I have held he was a competent witness, while there are some discrepancies in his statement, the evidence of Dr. Spence is consistent with Woodcock's statement and it is inconsistent with the confession of Ronald Moffatt."

Then, Justice Fuller got right to the point:

"Consideration of the evidence as a whole leaves me with reasonable doubt, in fact, I must say, a substantial doubt as to the guilt of Ronald Moffatt. He is entitled to the benefit of that doubt and I therefore find him not guilty of the offence for which he has been charged."

Moffatt was ordered to stand up.

"I have found you not guilty of the charge laid against

you, the charge to which you confessed to the police ... All I have to say to you is this. You of course yourself know whether your statement was true or not; if it was not true then you brought it upon yourself, all the trouble you have been in, in connection with this case, all the trouble given your parents, simply because you failed to tell the truth. I hope you will, at least, learn from this trial and you will never forget it," stated the judge.

And with that, Moffatt was told he could leave the courtroom.

The verdict was front page news in the press and a delightful shock to the defendant.

"When the judge at the then new Juvenile Court Building on Jarvis Street said that he found me to be innocent and I was free to go, it was like I was dreaming and was afraid to wake up. My heart was pounding so hard that I thought it was going to jump out of my chest. The elation I felt overwhelmed me. I ran around the courtroom shaking hands and even startled the Crown Attorney by offering to shake his hand, but I was hesitant to walk out of the courtroom because I was so used to being under escort that I felt that if I had that I would be subdued and put in restraints for trying to escape," states Moffatt.

After Bette Moffatt assured her boy that no one would shackle him for trying to leave the courthouse, Moffatt exited the building with his family. The Moffatts went back to Vanauley Street and tried to celebrate, but a flock of reporters soon descended at their door. Moffatt and his parents found themselves subjected to a seemingly endless round of interviews.

Ron, Omar and Bette Moffatt were not named in news coverage of the verdict and the post-release press conference on Vanauley Street. Ron was still a juvenile, so he was generally referred to in generic terms, as a "boy" or "teenager". The *Toronto Telegram* elected to use the pseudonym, "Bob Smith" whenever it quoted Moffatt.

Moffatt explained his story in detail to reporters. He said he went into hiding to avoid his father's wrath because he had been truant from school. It was simply a bad coincidence that Moffatt disappeared shortly after Mallette was murdered, the lead suspect in the case being a young teenage boy. When discovered in his hiding spot, Moffatt told the press he thought the arresting policemen were truant officers. Moffatt detailed his harrowing interrogation at the College Street police station. For the benefit of reporters, he repeated Detective Adolphus Payne's alleged threat: "If you don't tell us the truth, we'll get tough with you."

Moffatt said his confession was shaped by a combination of bullying tactics and leading questions. He also told the press that confessing was a foolish gambit to look like "a big shot."

Moffatt's parents seemed "happy at their son's release" but were "still angry over his conviction. Both mother and father considered him innocent from the start. His two lawyers, Mr. Knox and Pat Hartt considered him innocent from start to finish," reported the May 17 *Toronto Daily Star*.

In a front page story published that same day, the *Toronto Telegram* described Moffatt as "a well built, good looking boy with brown hair combed back in a wave" who "grinned self-consciously when he said he confessed to causing [Wayne Mallette's] death because, 'I wanted to get some kind of fame.'"

The *Telegram* also noted the boy's rough handling by police. While cops didn't "belt me around or anything" Moffatt said he was "scared they might" and was able to "piece together a convincing story" from the questions he was being asked.

Today, Moffatt wonders about some of the comments he made at his impromptu press conference. Moffatt was understandably nervous about being re-arrested, and says he didn't want to "upset or give the authorities any reason to be mad at me." So he took a share of blame, emphasizing the notion that his confession was in part motivated by some juvenile attempt at looking like a criminal big-shot.

Regardless of Moffatt's true state of mind, his parents didn't hold back. Bette Moffatt was particularly loquacious. She told reporters her son couldn't ride a bike—a key fact given the suspect in Mallette's death was seen on a bicycle. Bette complained that authorities took hours to inform her and Omar that their son was in custody. And she was bitter about the medical evidence used against her son: "[Bette Moffatt] said she could not understand how a dental witness at the first trial could testify there was no doubt that marks on Wayne Mallette came from her son's teeth ... At the second trial, she said, dentists established that the marks definitely came from another youth," reported the *Telegram*.

In some ways, this about-face on dental evidence wasn't that surprising. A recent report on the use of forensic science in criminal cases poured cold water all over bite-mark analysis. As presented to President Barack Obama, the report described bite-mark analysis as "scientifically unreliable."

"Bite-mark analysis does not meet the scientific standards for foundational validity, and is far from meeting such standards. To the contrary, available scientific evidence strongly suggests that examiners cannot consistently agree on whether an injury is a human bite-mark and cannot identify the source of bite-mark with reasonable accuracy," stated the report, from the President's Council of Advisors on Science and Technology.

Given this document was released September 2016, the state of bite-mark analysis in the mid-1950s can only be imagined.

Omar Moffatt said the trial had drastically depleted the family's already strained finances. Both parents wondered why Ron wasn't released on bail after Woodcock was arrested. For this, they blamed Inspector Payne. They accused the detective of holding onto their son long after it became clear he was innocent.

On a more positive note, Moffatt's parents were "both

deeply grateful to his lawyers, Pat Hartt and Albert Knox," stated the *Telegram*.

After countless interviews, Moffatt recalls he was "glad to see the reporters leave."

His family home was still packed with relatives and well-wishers, however, whom Moffatt felt obliged to thank for their support. Once he got the opportunity, he slipped outside and just walked and walked. The following morning, he got up and walked all the way to Scarborough—quite a distance from downtown Toronto—to visit his aunt, uncle and cousins. The ability to walk where he pleased, as long as he wanted, was an experience he relished.

If the Moffatts were delighted, Wayne Mallette's family was having a considerably tougher time of it.

Toronto Police files contain an exchange of letters between Wayne's father, John Mallette, and Detective Bernard Simmonds. A letter from the detective dated May 7, 1957, offered details about the time and place for Moffatt's second trial. Det. Simmonds informed Mallette that he and his son, Ronald would be required to attend.

A May 23 letter to Mallette detailed the aftermath of the retrial: "I understand that you were speaking on the telephone with Inspector A. Payne of this Department in regard to the disposition of this case and I feel sure that information was given you at that time and that the judgment given was explained ... Any inaccuracies that may have appeared in the press must be overlooked as this case was held in camera and the press and public were excluded, however, there was a lack of corroboratory evidence and sufficient doubt through medical evidence, etc., resulting in the finding giving," wrote Det. Simmonds.

The detective expressed sympathy for the Mallette family and encouraged John Mallette to write any time.

A follow-up letter from Mallette, dated June 3, expressed the depth of the man's confusion and anguish. In his neatly handwritten note, Mallette praised police for their investigation but made it clear he was baffled by the chain of events. He seemed devastated how one person could be convicted for killing his son, only for a new suspect to emerge. Mallette's letters reflect rage and a man shaken by grief.

Moffatt himself, while overjoyed to be released, was also bitter about the whole experience.

"At the end of my second trial (when I was acquitted), nobody said sorry or even offered any sort of an apology. The judge only said that from now on that underage suspects should have either a parent or lawyer present during the interrogation. Also, it was mentioned that I would not be receiving any kind of compensation. My lawyers had mentioned that they may file a civil suit but this never happened," he states.

Moffatt's observations about compensation are backed by news coverage at the time. While not entirely dismissing the idea of a civil action, Moffatt's lawyers weren't enthusiastic about the possibility.

"The boy's lawyer doubted if anything can be done to recompense him for time in jail. He said an action would be difficult because the lad was properly charged and proper means were followed. 'The main thing is justice has been done, even though it took quite a long time,' Mr. Knox said. "I was satisfied from the beginning he was innocent and worked to prove it,'" reported the *Star*.

Today, Moffatt regrets that his parents didn't pursue a lawsuit for compensation. He acknowledges, however, that they were ground down by the whole, horrible experience and wanted to put it behind them. His parents were also broke, which would make them wary about incurring further legal fees. Omar Moffatt was not making big money as a punch-press operator. Omar and Bette had been reduced to selling pieces of their furniture to pay legal bills.

If there were no formal apologies and compensation in the offing, Moffatt was also largely left to his own devices to fit back into society. The reintegration process did not go smoothly.

"I was mad at the world and very resentful of any kind of authority. I developed a short fuse and tried to be a tough guy," he says.

Understandably, Moffatt bore an intense fear of police. He had nightmares that cops were coming after him again. If he saw a patrolman on the street, he would turn around or walk away to avoid them.

To his later regret, Moffatt didn't return to school. Instead, he returned to former haunts in downtown

Toronto around Spadina Avenue and Queen Street. He reunited with former friends.

"Before I knew it, I had a new girlfriend and was hanging out with her and my old gang of buddies. It was hard to find work then as we were in the middle of a bad recession and I was too busy trying to make up for lost time and trying to have as much fun as possible," recalls Moffatt.

His circle of friends coalesced into something they dubbed the Joker Gang. Evidently, Moffatt's fear of police didn't prevent him from slipping back into petty thievery. The Joker Gang began breaking into restaurants for easy money. According to Moffatt, the Joker Gang was so brash, members would sometimes take the time to grill up hamburgers and hotdogs in restaurants they robbed. Such antics did not go unnoticed and eventually the members of the Joker Gang were caught by police. To Moffatt's horror, the crew was taken to the same College Street station where he'd been roughly interrogated by Detectives Payne and Simmonds. Three of the older boys in the Joker Gang were sent to juvenile detention. Moffatt and two others received probation.

Just as with Moffatt's earlier attempt at robbing the St. Lawrence Market with an older teen, his parents were furious at his illegal activities. A dressing down from Bette Moffatt ended Ron's involvement with the Joker Gang.

Moffatt might have left the juvenile criminal demimonde, but he couldn't escape the memories of his arrest, trial and incarceration. Being behind bars is generally awful for anyone, much less a juvenile accused of killing a child.

"After a while I started having emotional problems. I would have nightmares about what had happened to me and I found it harder and harder to cope. I finally told my probation officer about everything and he set up an interview with a psychologist at the Toronto Psychiatric Hospital and I agreed to be admitted," he states.

This was in July 1957.

Moffatt remained at the Toronto Psychiatric Hospital, a place he was very familiar with already, for roughly three months. Things were relatively okay, but then "one day I was really upset and threw a plate at one of the staff. Next thing I know I was shipped off to Whitby," he states.

The facility Moffatt refers to was the cheerfully named Ontario Hospital for the Insane, in Whitby, Ontario. Based next to Lake Ontario, the place first opened in World War One. Conceived as a mental health hospital, it served as a convalescent hospital for wounded soldiers then returned to civilian use in 1919. It reopened as a psychiatric unit that same year. By the time Moffatt got there, the Hospital for the Insane was routinely doling out newly developed anti-depressant and anti-psychotic drugs to disturbed patients. Like the Toronto Psychiatric Hospital in the same period, however, the Whitby facility still indulged in more radical treatment approaches. "Between 1948 and 1959, there were more than 300 leucotomy and lobotomy operations performed at Whitby," stated a hospital history.

A psychiatric facility with the more generic name, Ontario Shores Centre for Mental Health Sciences, currently occupies the site of the old Ontario Hospital for the Insane.

Moffatt didn't receive any brain surgery or mind-shattering treatments. The hospital staff did their best to help him cope with the intense anxiety, guilt, anger and stress he faced. At the time, it was understood that soldiers who had been in combat could suffer intense trauma for years afterwards. In the 1950s, this was referred to as "combat fatigue" or "battle shock". The condition is now called Post-Traumatic Stress Disorder or PTSD. The idea that civilians such as Moffatt could also experience PTSD from their own awful experiences wasn't well understood, however.

Moffatt describes his Whitby stay as follows: "More sessions with doctors and more nerve pills. I must say, I started feeling better and more relaxed. They understood that it was going to take a long time to get over my trauma but for my sake, I had to learn to cope with it and get on with life. I have, even though once and a while those old memories come around, usually in the form of nightmares."

Moffatt was released from the hospital in the spring of 1958.

"One day I was called into the administration office and was told I was being sent home with my grandparents. My grandfather helped me get a job at CCM in Weston and I was doing fine, but I was becoming a real loner. I got along great with the people I worked with, but most times when they asked me to do something after work or on the weekends I would make some excuse not to go. I would stay in my bedroom for hours and never come out," he recalls.

Moffatt once screwed up the courage to ask out an attractive girl who worked in the cafeteria. To his surprise, she agreed to go out with him. When the date-night arrived, however, Moffatt panicked and called her to cancel.

Eventually, Moffatt moved back in with his parents. At some point, he was contacted by *Toronto Daily Star* reporter Joe Scanlon. Scanlon was friendly and had Moffatt to his house for dinner, to discuss his case and find out what the boy had been up to since his acquittal. Scanlon was also helpful, arranging for Moffatt to get a job with the Canadian Broadcasting Corporation (CBC) Film Library in early 1959. Moffatt worked there for two years, then met a girl while on holiday with a friend. Her name was Dolly Marie, and her parents owned a farm in a tiny community called Muir, outside Woodstock, Ontario.

On May 20, 1961, Ron and Dolly got married. He was 19 years-old, she was only 16. The pair would eventually divorce after having three children, but remain good friends today.

"We both realize now that we were too young then to be getting married," recalls Moffatt.

Moffatt wasn't able to run away from his past, however.

After getting married, Moffatt and Dolly lived on

her parents' farm. The pair occupied the front part of the farmhouse. One day in the early 1960s, Moffatt stepped onto the yard only to be greeted by "a swarm of reporters" who "asked questions about my name being used in a book about Steven Truscott," he recalls.

Steven Truscott was a 14-year-old boy living on an air force based in Clinton, Ontario, who was accused, in June 1959, of raping and murdering a younger classmate, Lynne Harper. All the evidence against Truscott was circumstantial, but that didn't matter. After a lighting fast trial, the boy was convicted. Tried as an adult, Truscott was sentenced to hang. This was soon commuted to life in prison.

By the early 1960s, however, some observers began to sense that Truscott hadn't actually committed the crime for which he was imprisoned. One of the leading crusaders on his behalf was a female journalist named Isabel LeBourdais. LeBourdais carefully built up a strong case for Truscott's innocence. The results were published in a hugely controversial 1966 book, *The Trial of Steven Truscott*. The book was the first major step in a decades-long battle to clear Truscott's name.

Truscott's case has many bizarre parallels with Moffatt's story, not the least being that they were both 14-year-old kids in Ontario in the 1950s charged with the death of a child. Both were convicted, despite weak evidence. Bicycles played a major role in both cases (Truscott was the last person seen with Harper, giving her a lift on the handlebars of his bike to a highway where she allegedly began hitchhiking).

NATE HENDLEY

Another odd coincidence: in October 1966, prompted by LeBourdais' book, the Truscott case was reviewed by the Supreme Court of Canada. Assisting with Truscott's defence during the review was G. Arthur Martin, the same lawyer that Patrick Hartt worked for in the late 1950s when he defended Moffatt. Interestingly, while Hartt won Moffatt an acquittal, Martin was unsuccessful in getting the Supreme Court to overturn Truscott's conviction. Truscott would not be acquitted of murder until 2007, following a decision by the Ontario Court of Appeal.

According to Moffatt, LeBourdais wanted to include his story in her book. Moffatt at the time wanted nothing to do with this, however. While he had reluctantly spoken with reporters following his acquittal, by the 1960s, he just wanted to get on with his life the best he could and stop dwelling on his ordeal.

This was largely impossible though.

Moffatt had taken Justice Fuller's words about never forgetting his trial to heart, though probably not in the way the judge intended.

"I was changed. A friend of mine said, after [the trial and arrest] happened, that 14-year old boy died, and she was right. It changed me, completely changed me. I was depressed. A deep depression for a long, long time. I think the depression went on for 10 – 15 years," says Moffatt.

Chapter Eight - After the Acquittal

A few years after his acquittal, Ron Moffatt made a return visit to the Canadian National Exhibition. It was the first time he'd been there since 1956. He made the trip in the company of his wife, Dolly, and relatives.

"As soon as we entered the grounds all these bad feelings overcame me, and it was hard to remain on the site. However, we came upon the ride I had worked on that summer," he recalls.

Some of Moffatt's old co-workers recognized him and waved him over.

"They seemed genuinely happy to see me and offered the whole lot of us a tour and a free ride. So, the visit to the grounds ended up being both a happy and therapeutic experience. However, I never returned to the CNE again," says Moffatt.

As it turned out, the experience revisiting the CNE didn't prove sufficiently therapeutic to maintain his equilibrium.

"I did some follow-up therapy in my later years. Once in Sarnia in 1967 under the advice of my doctor,

I admitted myself to the psychiatric unit there for two months (I was more like a day patient as they let me out to go to work after two weeks). I attended group therapy and some sessions with a psychologist. My nerves got so bad they had to put me on nerve pills again and other medications because I started developing stomach ulcers," he recalls.

A similar situation occurred in 1972: "My ulcers got so bad that they perforated, and I ended up in the hospital for three months with tubes protruding from just about every orifice on my body. When I went in the hospital, I weighed 190 lbs. When I came out after the operation, I weighed 150 lbs. A few months later I was admitted to the psychiatric wing for three weeks for more group therapy and more nerve pills," says Moffatt.

His life was not all about psychiatric interventions, however. Moffatt had three children with Dolly: daughter, Cathy Anne Moffatt, son, Vernon Clifton Moffatt, and son Bradley Keith Moffatt.

In 1970, Moffatt moved to Sault Ste. Marie. He lived in Toronto and Edmonton for a while, then moved back to "the Soo" as it is known, where he has been ever since.

Ron and Dolly divorced March 23, 1972, but remain today on very good terms.

Life was rough for a few years following the split. Moffatt was troubled by alcohol, sadness, anger and pain. He describes this period as "a real tail spin." It was a spin he eventually climbed out of, with time and professional help.

Moffatt eventually earned his grade 12 high school equivalency, to make up for the years of education lost following his arrest. He took work as a caretaker in a Sault Ste. Marie school, for kids from kindergarten to grade eight. It was work he enjoyed. He recalls with delight how he loved to see children at the school grow up.

Moffatt got married a second time, in 1980, to a woman named Debbie Speers. They are still together, the marriage strong. Debbie worked as a registered practical nurse (RPN) at a local hospital.

In his spare time during his working life, Moffatt visited family and friends and read avidly. He never gave up his childhood interest in art. The Sault Ste. Marie School Board frequently relied on his talents for various art projects.

"One time they decided to enter a float in the local Communities Day Parade and asked me to design it. I was given a staff of five and two weeks at full salary to complete the float. The float won first prize. At one of the elementary schools, the principal asked me to do some cartoon drawings of the school and some of the students. I suggested that I do the drawings and have them projected onto the gym wall for the students to trace and paint. It turned out great and the local media came in and took pictures. They were shown on TV and in the local newspapers," says Moffatt.

Moffatt retired in 2007. His second wife had to retire as well, after developing Multiple Sclerosis (MS). Moffatt channelled his artistic sensibilities into cartooning.

NATE HENDLEY

"I used to do editorial cartoons for the local media and have done some private work for companies both in Canada and the USA. Presently, I only do cartoons for a local Internet site sootoday.com which appear every Sunday, it is called the Sunday Funny," he states.

"I keep busy, gardening, baking, and cooking up these exotic, weird meals. I help with the house cleaning and try and help the neighbours whenever they need it. I have a stepdaughter who is also now married (she's a school teacher) and she has a seven-year-old daughter (great kid, smart as a whip)," adds Moffatt.

His children from his first marriage are now all in middle-age and have their own kids. Moffatt remains in close contact with his children, visiting their families as often as possible.

Moffatt's own parents died in the mid-1990s, within six months of each other. Following Moffatt's acquittal, and the initial blast of media attention, his parents never wanted to discuss his ordeal. Moffatt describes his father, Omar, as "a loner" who "wasn't a talker." Bette Moffatt was the family conversationalist, but she too preferred to remain silent on what her son had gone through.

Not being able to discuss his trial, incarceration and retrial with his parents was painful, Moffatt admits.

But he can't begrudge their silence: "I love my parents. They went to bat for me. It made up for everything," he says.

While they "couldn't afford it" his parents paid for their son's legal costs, he adds. Moffatt deeply regrets there was no compensation with his case, to pay his parents back for all their financial help.

Asked to cite the worst moments of his ordeal, Moffatt offers the following: "First and foremost, being a scrawny 14-year-old old in an interrogation room with two hardened detectives trying to pry a confession out of me. The second was being in the detention area at Bowmanville, standing up all day and sleeping on the cold floor at night and that big redhead guard harassing me constantly. Third, being told by a guard that when I was old enough I could be taken to the Don Jail and hanged or the realization that I could be spending the rest of my life in prison."

Moffatt says he didn't realize he would be released once he turned 18, given his juvenile status.

Moffatt has worked hard to cope with the bitterness and anger generated by his experience.

"Other than having nightmares and the odd bad day when I read about somebody else's case similar to mine (and there have been so many), I have been fine and feel content with my life now. People that I haven't seen for years and are familiar with what happened to me in 1956 – 57, are surprised as well. I have kept myself together. One psychiatrist said he was surprised that I didn't end up a basket case," he says.

Following the Moffatt trial, lawyer Patrick Hartt went on to a stellar legal career. He earned much praise for his approach to the law. Writer and activist June Callwood described Hartt as "a gentle man with a capacity for reflection and idealism" in a May 28, 1986 *Globe* article.

One of Hartt's most famous cases took place in the fall of 1962, when he represented convicted killer Ronald Turpin in an appeal for clemency. The appeal was made to the Supreme Court of Canada, a last-ditch effort to prevent Turpin from being hanged. The Supreme Court rejected Hartt's appeal and Turpin was put to death for his crimes.

Shortly afterwards, Hartt was appointed to the Ontario Supreme Court—one of the youngest judges ever to obtain this post. The Ontario Supreme Court was merged in 1990 with other judicial bodies in the province.

A June 23, 1966 *Globe and Mail* article about the appointment cited Hartt's accomplishments. These included working with G. Arthur Martin and serving as counsel in a Royal Commission that looked into "the rise and fall of Windfall Oils and Mines Ltd."

The article mentioned that Hartt had been a special prosecutor in a trial involving Toronto art dealers selling fake Group of Seven paintings. The *Globe* also noted that "Mr. Hartt was involved in a prominent case nine years ago when he won freedom for a 15 year-old boy who had been convicted in juvenile court" for the death of Wayne Mallette. "Mr. Hartt won an acquittal for the youth, who had spent eight months in custody, when Peter Woodcock, 18, later admitted being responsible," added the *Globe*.

On April 1, 1971, Hartt was appointed Chairman of the Law Reform Commission of Canada (LRCC). A permanent body established by an Act of Parliament, the Commission led a review of Canadian law, with an eye towards improving and modernizing legal statutes. There was a focus on finding ways the law impacted disadvantaged groups.

As Chairman, Hartt made the front page of the *Toronto Star* on March 23, 1972, sharing space with a photograph of Prime Minister Pierre Trudeau. "Laws should be so simple people don't need lawyers," Hartt told the *Star*. In the same article, Hartt complained that the Canadian legal system was "too costly and too complex" for average citizens.

The Law Reform Commission issued its first annual report in August, 1972.

"Law reform is not a matter for lawyers alone. In modern society, there is virtually no individual life that is not affected and often in very serious ways, by our laws," stated one of the passages.

Hartt made the front page of the *Globe and Mail* on November 16, 1974, in an article that called him "disheartened". The story said Hartt was run down because no one seemed to be listening to the Law Reform Commission's recommendations on updating and simplifying the law.

In 1977, Hartt headed up Royal Commission on the Northern Environment. The commission was supposed to look into the impact of logging on First Nations people in Ontario. Hartt quit after a few months, in part because he was "shocked and horrified by the strength of the anti-Indian feeling he found among a few whites when he held hearings in the northwest," according to the April 5, 1978 *Toronto Star*.

Hartt served on the Ontario Court of Justice (General Division) from 1990 – 1999 then on the Superior Court of Justice from 1999 – 2001.

Hartt made news when he ruled in a case involving the appointment of two additional transit commissioners by Toronto City Council.

"In his ruling yesterday, Judge Hartt found that council acted improperly because it ignored a section of the City of Toronto Act that requires that the appointment of TTC commissioners be supported by a two-thirds vote of council," reported the June 30, 1999 *Globe*.

Three years later, Hartt was back in the news again, for his role in an Ontario Review Panel that examined the case of a psychiatric patient named Scott Starson.

Hartt currently resides in a seniors facility. His contact information is not publicly available. In response to a query I made, the Office of the Chief Justice (the one organization that seemed to know Hartt's whereabouts) attempted to get in touch with Hartt, to pass on an interview request. The Office left voicemail messages and wrote Hartt a letter. So far, the elderly Hartt has not replied.

Moffatt never saw Hartt again after his acquittal but remains extremely grateful for his services and passion.

Toronto Police Inspector Adolphus Payne who led Moffatt's arrest and interrogation, also had an illustrious career. He rose to the rank of staff superintendent, retiring in February 1974, having been on the force for over four decades.

Payne's retirement was front-page news in Toronto. The February 7, 1974 *Toronto Star* ran side-by-side front page photographs of Payne as a young man in police uniform (complete with an English 'bobby' style hat) and wiping away a tear at a retirement dinner. The article referred to him as "Canada's greatest detective" and detailed his mission to bring Edwin Boyd to justice.

The *Star* piece contained an ironic observation, from none other than G. Arthur Martin, who had gone from being a highly-regarded criminal lawyer to an Ontario Court of Appeal justice.

"I don't remember ever winning a case when Dolph Payne was in charge of it. He was a very brilliant detective and contributed to making Toronto police one of the greatest police forces of the world," stated Martin.

Payne's death in 1981 was also big news.

"Adolphus J. Payne, long regarded as Canada's greatest detective, died today in Port Hope General Hospital. He was 72. He became a national hero for breaking up the notorious Boyd Gang of bank robbers in 1952," wrote legendary crime reporter Gywn "Jocko" Thomas in the July 8, 1981 *Toronto Star*.

Payne's partner in the Moffatt case, Bernard Simmonds, also enjoyed a long, successful police career. He rose to become Metro Deputy Police Chief, the second highest position on the Metropolitan Toronto police force. As Deputy Police Chief, he oversaw the detective division, among other duties. A *Toronto Star* article on his retirement in January 1976, described Simmonds as "a crack homicide investigator for many years." Simmonds died in Toronto following a short illness, on June 28, 1991. His obituary, the next day in the *Star*, noted that Simmonds was part of "Toronto's first full-time homicide squad."

The deceased policemen cannot speak to what went on in the College Street police station the day Ronald Moffatt was interrogated.

Henry Herbert Bull, the intense Crown Attorney who drove Moffatt to tears on the witness stand, worked in the judicial system for 30 years.

After Moffatt's retrial, Bull continued to aggressively prosecute cases. His most famous case, arguably, was that of Arthur Lucas, the man he successfully prosecuted for a double homicide in 1962.

Bull moved on to become Crown Attorney for Metropolitan Toronto and York County. In this position, he directed the work of some 30 assistant Crown Attorneys. During his career, Bull also served as president of the Canadian Crown Attorneys Association and was a bencher (that is, a member of the board of directors) of the Law Society of Upper Canada.

In the mid-1960s, Bull "was distinguished as one of two Canadian lawyers to be asked to lecture at a short course for prosecutors at Chicago's Northwestern University," reported the September 4, 1968 *Globe and Mail*.

Interestingly enough, the other lawyer asked to lecture in Chicago was Bull's close friend, G. Arthur Martin.

Bull earned respect, from the press and his peers, for his sharp legal mind and insightful arguments.

"...as the Crown's representative, Bull was most characterized by his tough and remorseless advocacy. Defence counsel couldn't expect a break from Henry Bull and judges needed to stay on their toes," noted the book, *Learned Friends*.

Bull's forceful character extended outside of the courtroom. He "did not hesitate to criticize others when he believed they were wrong ... Last November, he told a Commons committee that any evils in the Canadian bail system were not a fault of the law but arise from poor administration by officials ... In an address to an Osgoode Hall audience in 1966, Mr. Bull insisted that trials should continue to be public but that the press should improve its coverage," wrote the *Globe*.

Bull wasn't always hard-nosed however. In 1965, he complained that courtroom overcrowding in Toronto was causing defendants awaiting trial to languish in the city's grim Don Jail. He suggested a Royal Commission be struck to look into this situation.

In 1968, Bull suffered a heart attack at work. It was a reoccurrence of cardiac problems that had landed him in hospital for three months a few years previously. This time, however, Bull didn't recover. Rushed from his Toronto office, he died on September 3 before reaching the hospital.

Write-ups in the major newspapers were highly respectful.

"When we had occasion to engage him in dispute, as happened a number of times over the years, it was with awareness that we were grappling with a good, dedicated and resourceful adversary," stated the *Globe* the day after Bull's death.

The *Star's* obituary, published September 4, 1968, quoted several luminaries praising Bull. Among their ranks was the ubiquitous G. Arthur Martin (described as a "friend of 33 years").

"If Henry Bull hadn't been a lawyer, he would have been a great artist. He had an excellent sense of the dramatic. He was a man of artistry and a superb cross-examiner. He had the reputation of being tough, but he was a great humanist," said Martin.

Like much of downtown Toronto, Vanauley Street has changed drastically. The old, rickety cold-water flats have been replaced by sturdy townhomes and condos. In the mid-1960s, a huge public housing project called Alexandra Park opened just north of where the Moffatt family used to reside. In recent years, a massive revitalization initiative has been underway to make Alexandra Park more aesthetically pleasing. Some old units were torn down in February 2014, with construction of new rental townhomes and private market condominiums commencing later that same year.

A huge condominium development, scheduled for completion in 2019, is going up at 80 Vanauley. The SQ 2 Condos development will feature over 150 suites spread out among 14 storeys. Amenities include a fitness room, roof top deck complete with garden and hot tub, and 24-hour security and concierge. Suites have been priced at around $900,000.

Vanauley Street has not entirely lost its old grittiness, however. The Toronto Vanauley Street YMCA Centre, at 7 Vanauley, offers an emergency shelter for young, homeless men, age 16 – 24. And many of the residences on the street are run by Toronto Community Housing (TCH—the city's public housing authority).

The Ontario Training School for Boys, Bowmanville, was renamed Pine Ridge School in 1967. The facility was closed in 1979. In 2013, the site was placed on The Canadian Register of Historic Places (CRHP), which lists buildings and locales with heritage value. Bowmanville made the cut for the progressive spirit in which it was launched, its Prairie School-style architecture and for housing German prisoners in World War Two.

The Ontario Training School for Boys, Bowmanville,

was cited in a front page story in the *Toronto Star*, December 10, 2017, but not because of its historic architecture. The facility was named in an investigative report detailing 220 legal settlements made between the Ontario government and former residents of a dozen training schools the province once ran. These legal settlements—kept secret for decades—involved payouts, sometimes amounting to hundreds of thousands of dollars for abuse residents allegedly endured from staff and teachers. The last training school in Ontario closed in 1984.

In their lawsuits, students claimed a litany of horrors including sexual assaults, beatings, psychological torture, being compelled by guards to fight each other, extended periods in solitary confinement, not being allowed to use the washroom until they soiled themselves, etc.

The article included photographs of the abandoned Bowmanville/Pine Ridge facility.

"Today, the former site of Pidge Ridge, which opened in 1925 as the Bowmanville Boys' Training School, sits derelict. Buildings that housed hundreds of children for half-a-century are now boarded up, overgrown with weeds and covered in graffiti. No trespassing signs and security cameras warn passerby to keep away," wrote the December 10, 2017 *Star*.

One day after the article ran, a pair of law firms commenced a joint class action lawsuit against the Province of Ontario on behalf of abused training school students. The Ontario Training School for Boys, Bowmanville/Pine Ridge was one of 12 institutions cited in the suit, which was launched by Koskie Minsky of Toronto and Watkins Law of Thunder Bay.

The Ontario Reformatory, Guelph, became the Guelph Correctional Centre. It was shut down in 2002. Many of the original buildings still exist and tours can be arranged to see the facility. The location is a popular hiking spot.

The main functions of the Toronto Psychiatric Hospital were taken over by the new Clarke Institute of Psychiatry, which opened in 1966 on College Street in downtown Toronto. The Clarke merged with three other facilities in 1998 to become the Centre for Addiction and Mental Health (CAMH).

The Ontario Hospital for the Insane in Whitby, Ontario is still functioning, albeit under a blander name. It is currently called the Ontario Shores Centre for Mental Health Services.

The Metro Theatre at 677 Bloor Street West, where Ron Moffatt watched a double feature the night Wayne Mallette was murdered, went from showing B-films and second-run flicks in the 1950s to primarily screening porn in the 1970s. As years went on, and adult film connoisseurs began to embrace video porn viewed in the privacy of their homes, the Metro became a relic of the past. By the early 2000s, it had the dubious distinction of being the last large-size, public cinema in Toronto primarily screening adult films. The Metro closed in 2013 and the space was turned over to other uses. It is currently a flourishing indoor climbing gym.

The Canadian National Exhibition (CNE) remains as popular as ever. The 2016 version of the "Ex" drew over 1.5 million people from August 19 – September 5. This marked the second-best attendance in roughly two decades. The 2016 CNE also featured 1,085 performers, 700 vendors and exhibitors, 140 animals at the CNE farm, 114 games and 62 rides.

Peter Woodcock, the killer who put Moffatt behind bars, spent decades in psychiatric care and somehow managed to commit one final murder. He talked openly about his crimes with a variety of interviewers, though he never really explained why he decided to become a serial killer. Some of Woodcock's interviews can be seen on YouTube, for viewers with strong stomachs.

Woodcock resided at the Oak Ridge branch of the maximum-security Penetanguishene Mental Health Centre most of his adult life. He seemed to cope well with institutionalization, having lots of sex with male inmates and establishing little routines that suited his needs.

Woodcock became a very unlikely subject in various revolutionary treatment initiatives in the 1960s and 70s, including LSD-therapy. He also sampled several other powerful drugs and took part in an off-the-wall experiment involving something called the "Total Encounter Capsule".

"The basic idea was that stripping away distractions from the outside world would reveal the core of goodness that is well-hidden in the average murderous psychopath ... The capsule was a soundproof, windowless, perpetually lit 8-by-10-foot room at the Oak Ridge maximum-security mental hospital in Ontario ... It was the brainchild of a young psychiatrist, Elliott Barker. Inmates, stripped naked and pumped full of LSD, uppers and truth serum, would be locked in for days to bare their innermost feelings," reported a *New York Daily News* story published November 30, 2013.

It was hoped these deviants would develop empathy through intimacy and soul bearing dialogues with their peers. Many of these sessions were filmed.

A television documentary entitled, *A Bad Trip*, aired by the Canadian Broadcasting Corporation (CBC) in late 1997, examined Oak Ridge patient Steve Smith's experience in the Total Encounter Capsule. Smith was a late 1960s-era hippie-drifter who wound up at Oak Ridge after stealing a car. As part of his therapy, he was given mind-shattering drugs and handcuffed to Peter Woodcock. Apparently, Woodcock was supposed to act as a guide, steering Smith through his drug haze to some kind of enlightenment. Instead, Woodcock spent most of his time boasting about his crimes, Smith told CBC.

Unsurprisingly, the Total Encounter Capsule failed miserably when it came to healing Woodcock, though that wouldn't become evident for a few more years. While the exact nature of Woodcock's dysfunction remains a mystery, he never expressed any regret for his murders.

In the early 1980s, Woodcock legally changed his name

NATE HENDLEY

to David Michael Krueger. A couple years after this name-change, the first of the *Nightmare on Elm Street* movies was released, featuring a sadistic killer named Freddy Krueger. Unless Woodcock was clairvoyant, the similarity in names seems to have been merely a sick coincidence.

Woodcock's articulate nature and obvious intelligence fooled some people into thinking he was getting better. In September 1989, he was transferred to the medium-security Brockville Psychiatric Hospital, where he was granted a remarkable degree of leniency. He was taken on a tour of a local railway museum by hospital staff. More astonishingly, Woodcock was allowed out to see the movie *Silence of the Lambs*. That 1991 thriller saw Anthony Hopkins playing a brilliant but evil murderer questioned by an FBI agent for insights in tracking down a serial killer at large.

Over the decades, Woodcock never lost his own desire to kill. He also honed his ability to manipulate, as noted by author Jon Ronson in the book, *The Psychopath Test*. The book cited Woodcock's time in the Total Encounter Capsule and other forms of unusual therapy. Such methods simply "taught him how to be a more devious psychopath," wrote Ronson. Woodcock learned how to fake empathy and keep his more maniacal impulses and thoughts to himself. Unfortunately, authorities found this out far too late.

In the early 1990s, Woodcock became close friends with Bruce Hamill, a former psychiatric patient at Penetanguishene. Hamill had spent over a decade in mental health facilities after being found not guilty, by reason of insanity, of murder. The murder victim was an elderly Ottawa woman whom Hamill stabbed more than 35 times. Following years of therapy, Hamill was deemed cured, more or less, and released. He obtained a job as a security officer at a courthouse in Ottawa (which showed the frightening degree of faith people put in his rehabilitation).

Woodcock sensed Hamill was still deeply disturbed and easily pushed around. Woodcock spun a tale about an international/intergalactic alien brotherhood that could somehow rescue Hamill from his psychiatric plight. However, the alien brethren would only arrive if Hamill was willing to kill another Brockville inmate named Dennis Kerr.

On July 13, 1991, Woodcock received a day-pass, allowing him to come and go from the Brockville Psychiatric Hospital. The pass was good for three hours. Staff anticipated Woodcock would use it to go into town, buy some pizza and savour his freedom in other low-key ways. Woodcock had different plans. He was signed out by his buddy, Hamill. The pair enticed Kerr to a lonely location in the woods, then killed him with a knife and other weapons Hamill purchased earlier that day. The two stabbed Hamill repeatedly then had sex with him when he was dead.

After that, Hamill and Woodcock went their separate ways. Hamill tossed back a bunch of sleeping pills, to knock himself out in anticipation of the aliens' arrival and his removal to their world. Woodcock strolled to a local police station, blood on his shirt, and confessed to murder. Police raced to the crime scene where they found a very dead Kerr and a very out of it Hamill. At the police station Woodcock masturbated in his cell, in full view of all, then repeated the act at a hospital and county jail

In the *Bad Trip* documentary, Woodcock is asked by a CBC reporter about Kerr's murder. Woodcock by this point is bald and wears big clunky glasses, shorts and a green plaid shirt. He is notably paunchy. He looks like a middle-aged accountant, but his conversation is searing.

"For me it was the last hurrah. It was like a physical sensual excitement. And I was the one who pulled down the trousers to make it look like a sex crime. But it was not a sex crime," Woodcock tells the interviewer.

Q. "Why did you do that?"

(Woodcock): "Just to confuse the authorities."

Q. "What did you do to make it look like a sex crime?"

(Woodcock): "I stabbed him in various rather personal parts of the anatomy."

The episode with Hamill marked the end of any attempt to reintroduce Woodcock to society. He was returned to Oak Ridge, something that annoyed him at first. In 1994, the Ontario Court of Appeal turned down a request by Woodcock to be transferred to a psychiatric institution outside of Ontario. Woodcock claimed he felt unsafe at Oak Ridge and would have better treatment options elsewhere.

The Court of Appeal hearing was notable for some

blunt commentary about Woodcock's character. His own lawyer, Greg Brodsky, described him as a "very dangerous fellow" reported the July 9, 1994 *Globe and Mail*.

That was mild compared to a report made by a psychiatrist named Angus McDonald. Woodcock, wrote McDonald, "appears extremely dangerous, perhaps one of the worst sexual psychopaths I have ever observed in my forensic experience," stated the *Globe*.

In the end the Court of Appeal decided Woodcock would be fine at Oak Ridge. Woodcock remained at this facility the rest of his life. During his years there, Woodcock was interviewed by crime reporter Mark Bourrie. Bourrie's revelations were published in a startling book called *By Reason of Insanity*, in 1997.

Bourrie possibly got to know Woodcock better than anyone, except perhaps hospital staff. The most obvious question Bourrie posed was, why?

"In his careful, soft-spoken voice, he sometimes tried to explain why he killed but he never came up with rational reasons," wrote Bourrie in the *Toronto Star*, March 9, 2010.

In a 1993 interview with Bourrie, however, Woodcock came close to offering a reason, such as it was, for his actions: "I'm accused of having no morality, which is a fair assessment, because my morality is whatever the system allows," said Woodcock.

Under the name David Krueger, Woodcock took part

in a BBC documentary that eventually aired in 2002 under the title, *Mind of a Murderer: The Mask of Sanity*.

When it came to discussing the Carole Voyce murder, Woodcock said, "I felt like God. The power of God over another human being. I didn't feel any sense of remorse or guilt at that time, I just wanted to correct a balance. Two boys had died, so maybe now a girl should die."

The BBC interviewer then asked Woodcock why he wanted to feel like God.

Woodcock's reply: "It was the pleasure it gave me. I got very little pleasure from anything else in life. But in the strangling of children I found a degree and a sensation of pleasure. And of accomplishment. Because it was such a good feeling I wanted to duplicate it. And so I went out to seek duplication."

Q. "People would be horrified to hear you view it as an accomplishment."

(Woodcock): "I know, but I'm sorry, this is not meant for sensitive ears. This is a terrible recitation. But I'm being as honest as I can."

Later Woodcock is asked about the Kerr murder.

(Woodcock): "I just wanted to know what it would feel like to kill somebody."

Q. "But you'd already killed three people.

(Woodcock): "Yes, but that was years and years and years and years ago."

Canadian TV producer Alan Echenberg also took part in an interview with Woodcock at the Oak Ridge facility.

At the time of the interview, Woodcock was "a half-blind, overweight, poorly dressed and otherwise non-descript old man—nobody's stereotype of a monstrous killer," wrote Echenberg in the *Ottawa Jewish Bulletin*, November 8, 2010.

Nonetheless, Woodcock made a deeply disturbing impression on the producer.

"I sat in a room with him for hours as he talked to the interviewer calmly, with obvious intelligence and in great detail—but completely matter-of-factly—about the gruesome acts he had committed ... It would have been easier to understand and digest, maybe, if Woodcock had been more of a stereotypical monster—a barking psychotic with an evil grin and a threatening demeanour ... Instead, he was a pale, lumpy old guy to whom you wouldn't give a second look if you saw him on a bus or in a shopping mall," stated Echenberg.

In an interview for this book, Bourrie was asked to sum up Woodcock's character. Bourrie described him as "a small, unobtrusive little man. The banality of evil."

In a horrible irony, Woodcock's lack of remorse directly led to Ron Moffatt's release from prison. Woodcock's testimony was one the key reasons Moffatt was acquitted at his retrial.

At the time, Moffatt had spent eight months in custody "and might have stayed there the rest of his life but for a courtroom appearance by Peter Woodcock," noted the May 17, 1957 *Toronto Telegram*.

In the decades following his trial, however, there

were occasional questions about whether Woodcock was being completely truthful. Some of his therapists wondered if Woodcock really did kill Wayne Mallette. At Oak Ridge, Woodcock could be evasive about the topic or claim he didn't have time to kill the boy, given his Saturday night job at Casa Loma.

During one of their frequent conversations, Bourrie decided to put the matter directly to the convicted killer.

"One day in the summer of 1996, when Krueger phoned me to chatter about something trivial, I decided to ask him if he killed Wayne. He was in a rather jovial mood, happier than he had been in several weeks. The hospital had issued an edict earlier in the summer that he quit telling jokes to other patients. That rule had been lifted. ... So, did he kill Wayne Mallette? ... 'Oh, yes,' he said ... Why did he bother helping [Moffatt] get out of jail ... 'I was really angry that he was taking credit for something I did. It had bothered me since he was arrested, but I couldn't exactly come forward, could I?'" wrote Bourrie in *By Reason of Insanity*.

Woodcock died March 5, 2010, in Penetanguishene, a strange, fussy baby turned into a strange, fussy killer.

No one seemed too upset by his passing.

"I never had a chance to speak with Peter Woodcock as he was kept under tight security and was hustled into the court room and when finished testifying, hustled out. Should I have had the chance to talk with him I would have declined as this man was a very sick, deranged individual and I do not believe he had any remorse for the damage he caused to the victims' families or to mine. I do not think because of his mental illness he was capable of remorse," says Moffatt today.

Chapter Nine – Why Innocent People Confess

Justice Harold Fuller didn't understand why Ron Moffatt would make a false confession. Even while acquitting Moffatt, the judge took the time to scold the teen for not telling the truth. To this day, many people simply can't believe someone would confess to a crime they didn't commit. It happens, however, with alarming regularity, a fact astute observers have long understood.

"Confession is Not Proof of Guilt" read the headline of an editorial in the *Toronto Daily Star* that appeared shortly after Moffatt's acquittal.

"Laymen sometimes wonder why there is so much dispute in the courts about confessions. The clearing of a 15-year-old boy who had admitted killing Wayne Mallette, seven, gives a luminous answer. Here is the strongest sort of proof that confessions given to police should be viewed with some caution and not taken as absolute proof of guilt ... In this case, the juvenile later repudiated his confession, yet he might have remained a prisoner for life had it not been for the capture of Peter Woodcock after the Carole Voyce murder. Information given by Woodcock cleared the 15-year-old boy of the Mallette slaying," wrote the *Star*.

The editorial continued: "The boy's statement that he confessed because, 'I wanted to get some kind of fame' indicates at least that his statement was not obtained by police pressure or bullying—suspicion of which is a frequent cause of defense counsel contesting the admissibility of confessions as evidence. There remains the possibility that the police did not try as hard as they should have to check the facts against the boy's story. That is the danger about confessions—they represent the easy way to get a conviction. As this case shows, the easy way can also be the inaccurate way, giving rise to [a] grave miscarriage of justice."

While Moffatt might dispute there was no bullying during his interrogation, the editorial points to the importance of confessions in securing convictions. Even today, an admission of guilt remains a potent weapon for any prosecutor

"They call the confession 'the Queen of the Evidentiary Chess Board'. [Confessions are] not as powerful as DNA but way more satisfying—putting someone in jail on their words," states Osgoode Hall Law Professor Alan Young, in an interview.

Powerful, satisfying—and sometimes untrue.

"If all confessions could be accepted at their face value, no harm would be done. But it is not unusual for innocent people to confess to crimes they did not commit. Some do it for notoriety, others because they are too frightened or ignorant to know what they are doing. Some because they have been 'brainwashed' by police questioning," stated a follow-up editorial in the *Star* published October 11, 1958.

The editorial cited Moffatt's "discredited confession" in reminding readers of a simple point: just because a suspect says they did something, don't presume they did.

A U.S. study examined 250 cases, starting in 1989, in which DNA evidence exonerated someone convicted of a serious crime. In 16 percent of the cases, the suspect had made a false confession. In other words, they admitted to crimes science says they didn't commit.

These findings were included in a 2011 book, *Convicting the Innocent* by Brandon L. Garrett. When Garrett recently updated his work, the number of DNA exonerations leapt to 325. The rate of false confessions among this new total increased to 27 percent.

Prof. Young has written a paper that looked at wrongful convictions in the Canadian court system. According to his report, which is dated December 2016, there have been 28 documented wrongful convictions in Canada since the late 1980s. No doubt, the undocumented rate is much higher. Prof. Young isn't sure how common it is for Canadian suspects to make unfounded admissions of guilt. He does say, however, that "we are now seeing the phenomenon [of false confessions] rear its head" in Canada.

As a prime example, Prof. Young's paper cited the case of Romeo Phillion.

Phillion was a petty criminal in Ottawa who was arrested in 1972 for the armed robbery of a cab-driver. For a variety of ill-considered reasons, Phillion confessed to killing Leopold Roy, an Ottawa firefighter who had been stabbed to death in 1967. While Phillion had been a suspect in that killing, he had a solid alibi (he wasn't in town the night Roy was murdered) and was never charged. Phillion quickly recanted his confession but the damage was done.

In court, Phillion's lawyer said his client was antisocial and lied to feel important. It was suggested Phillion had a rather hare-brained scheme to collect reward money for the murder or just thought it was amusing to toy with the police. No matter. The jury convicted Phillion November 7, 1972 and he was sentenced to life.

Once in prison, Phillion loudly proclaimed he wasn't guilty. And he had a good case too; evidence emerged that Ottawa police knew Phillion wasn't in the city the day Roy died. Phillion got in touch with the Innocence Project.

Co-founded by Prof. Young in 1997, the Innocence Project aims to free individuals who have been wrongfully convicted. Based out of Osgoode Hall Law School, the organization typically handles four or five cases a year (out of hundreds of applications). Young is currently the director.

For the Phillion case, the Innocence Project joined forces with another Toronto-based group doing similar work called the Association in Defence of the Wrongly Convicted (AIDWYC). Now known as Innocence

Canada, AIDWYC helped Steven Truscott clear his name. In 2003, the two organizations filed an application with the Justice Minister to review Phillion's case, with an eye towards determining if he had been wrongfully convicted.

Authorities released Phillion from prison on bail as the application was reviewed. In August 2006, it was decided to re-open his case. Three years later, the Ontario Court of Appeal overturned Phillion's original conviction and called for a new trial. In April 2010, the Crown withdrew charges against Phillion for the Roy murder. There would be no retrial: Phillion was a free man in the eyes of the law, no longer burdened by a criminal record for murder. Unfortunately, Phillion died of emphysema only five years after the Crown's decision.

Just as with Moffatt, Phillion's initial confession, followed by a quick retraction, left a lot of people scratching their heads.

"Why would anyone ever admit doing a terrible crime they didn't do?" asked Professor Samuel Gross of the University of Michigan Law School, in a May 21, 2012 article posted on www.msnbc.com.

Prof. Gross had a ready answer to this perplexing question: "The first thing to note is the risk of false confessions goes up rapidly when the suspects are either juveniles or mentally handicapped or both," he stated.

Other reasons for making false admissions of guilt

include "low-esteem, being mentally challenged, psychosis and attention seeking," adds Prof. Young.

The www.msnbc.com story concerned a study Prof. Gross conducted using information from the National Registry of Exonerations database. The database tracks exonerations of wrongly convicted individuals, starting in 1989. It is maintained by the Center on Wrongful Convictions, a venture run by the Northwestern University School of Law and the University of Michigan Law School. In total, Prof. Gross examined 873 exonerations that took place between January 1989 and February 2012. Of this sample group, the professor found 135 cases in which suspects had made false confessions—only to be cleared later of any wrongdoing.

Police tactics play a huge role in generating phony admission of guilt.

Former Washington D.C. police detective James Trainum, has written an entire book about the subject, entitled *How the Police Generate False Confessions*.

Trainum makes the rather obvious point that being interrogated by police is a deeply unsettling experience for the person being questioned. Most suspects want to get the interrogation over with as soon as possible. Questioning can last hours, even days, and be exhausting as well as terrifying. Some suspects confess falsely to crimes they didn't commit just to bring the process to an end.

Other times, suspects are tricked into making confessions through the use of leading questions, or are 'fed' details about the crime in question. The goal is to get a suspect to "fill in the blanks" and admit to a narrative constructed by police. Moffatt experienced this technique first-hand. This tactic is particularly effective when the suspect is befuddled by drugs, drink or mental illness, and has difficulty remembering much of anything. Suspects in such a condition are more likely to agree to suggestions by police about their whereabouts and actions than more sober-minded, clear-thinking suspects.

Rougher interrogation techniques include denying a suspect food, water, sleep or bathroom breaks. Suspects may not be told their rights or threatened with violence. Physically beating a confession out of a suspect is fortunately rare in North America today, though it does occasionally occur. Violence doesn't have to involve punching and beating, however. Suspects are sometimes forced into uncomfortable positions for long periods of time (by say, handcuffing their wrist to an overhead pipe, forcing them to stand on their toes) or put into very cold or very hot spaces.

The so-called "Reid Technique"—a widely popular interrogation protocol for police across North America—has also been criticized for inducing false confessions. As developed by polygraph expert John Reid, the Reid procedure "consists of a structured nine-step process comprised of confrontation and minimization strategies. The former entails forceful accusations, the presentation of evidence (either real *or* manufactured) and interruptions whenever denials are attempted by the suspect. *Minimization* involves the sympathetic presentation of moral justifications or explanations for the crime, often accompanied by the implication that a confession will result in leniency," explained a 2011 article in *Criminal Law Quarterly* entitled, "Justice Imperiled: False Confessions and the Reid Technique".

Police utilizing the Reid Technique are also encouraged to observe "behavioral cues" including "facial expressions, eye contact, posture, hand gestures, particular phrases" etc. on the part of the suspect that supposedly point to guilt, stated the article. The problem is, no one has come up with a foolproof method of 'detecting' deceit just from talking to someone. Far from being a handy method to determine guilt, the Reid Technique has been criticized for encouraging false confessions.

"The interrogation is not investigative in nature; rather it is guilt-presumptive. Its purpose is to elicit a confession from a suspect who is 'known' or strongly suspected to be guilty," stated the *Criminal Law Quarterly* article.

As noted by just about everyone, false confessions are also common when the suspect isn't an adult. Suspects under 18 "are typically more impulsive, less mature and less able to weigh risks and consequences, and more vulnerable to pressures such as are found in the interrogation room," wrote Trainum.

Juvenile suspects tend to be more gullible and trusting than their adult counterparts as well. This leaves them prone to making false admissions.

During Moffatt's second trial, Judge Fuller suggested police only take statements from juveniles in the presence of their parents or a trusted adult. Another proposal is to mandate that lawyers be present whenever a young offender is questioned at a police station. The U.S. Supreme Court suggested as much, decades ago.

"The juvenile needs the assistance of counsel to cope with problems of law, to make skilled inquiry into the facts, to insist upon regularity of the proceedings and to ascertain whether he has a defence and to prepare and submit it. The child requires the guiding hand of counsel at every step in the proceedings against him," stated the court, in a 1967 ruling.

The last line in this statement is particularly important. The Supreme Court is saying young offenders need the guidance of attorneys throughout the entire legal process, from interrogation to trial.

Unfortunately, this sensible recommendation has never been implemented.

At present, "no [U.S.] state guarantees lawyers for every child during interrogation and only one state requires it under limited circumstances," noted a May, 2017 report from the National Juvenile Defender Center in the U.S.

The situation in Canada is no different.

"There is no entitlement for lawyers to be present during interrogations" with young offenders, says Prof. Young.

The Youth Criminal Justice Act does state that, "a young person has the right to retain and instruct counsel without delay, and to exercise that right personally, at any stage of proceedings against the young person."

Being able to request a lawyer, however, and having one present any time police question a juvenile are two different things.

Mandating the presence of lawyers—or at least, parents or an adult family member—when interrogating young offenders might lower the incidence of false confessions from deluded kids. Such precautions would benefit both the suspect and the legal system in general.

To see what happens when such measures aren't in place, the case of New York City's Central Park Five is a good place to start. The Five were a group of African-American and Hispanic teenagers, aged 14 and 15, arrested in April 1989 on charges stemming from the brutal physical and sexual assault of a white, female jogger. The victim was found, battered, unconscious and nearly lifeless in Central Park.

The underage suspects were interrogated by police for over a day, without parents or lawyers present. Police allegedly denied them food, water and sleep. Four of the accused ended up making videotaped confessions. Little evidence beyond these confessions linked the teens to the crime.

The case, which took place during a vicious crime wave in New York City, sparked outrage—mostly against the suspects. In May 1989, then real-estate mogul Donald Trump took out full page ads in *The New York Times* and other New York newspapers, denouncing "roving bands of wild criminals" and "murderers" who made it impossible for ordinary citizens to enjoy a walk in the park or feel secure in their homes. The ad called for the reinstatement of tough policing and the death penalty in New York State. The notices didn't explicitly refer to the Central Park Five, but the implication was clear.

The Five were convicted, almost entirely on the basis of their videotaped admissions of guilt. All were given stiff sentences. Years went by. Then, it was discovered that DNA evidence tied another suspect to the crime. By contrast, there were no traces of any DNA from the Central Park Five on the victim. The new suspect was jailed, the members of the Five who were still behind bars were released. In 2014, the group received $41 million in restitution by the state of New York.

Even without DNA, a court might have eventually tossed the original verdict against the Central Park Five. When examined in a more objective light, the boys' videotaped confessions seemed very shaky.

"So powerful that they persuaded two juries who had heard almost no other evidence—[the confessions] were actually so full of discrepancies and errors regarding the rape, even about where, when and how it took place and who was involved, as to make the statements implausible as evidence of the rape," noted the December 6, 2002 *New York Times.*

Such is the clout of a confession, however, that they can override all scientific evidence in some people's minds. When campaigning for president in 2016, Trump was asked about his incendiary ads. Did he regret publishing them? Not at all, said Trump. He insisted the Central Park Five were still guilty. After all, they confessed, didn't they?

Fortunately, not everyone is so obtuse on such matters. In a 1954 address to a police school, G. Arthur Martin discussed the role confessions play in investigations.

To those gathered, Martin stated:

"The next and perhaps the place where most cases break down are cases where confessions are sought to be introduced into evidence. Firstly, I would like to suggest to you as police officers, that you should not rely too much on confessions. If you have a confession from a person, it is only natural that you may be lulled into a false feeling of security that you have a strong case and you may be inclined to overlook other evidence that might be available to you if you did not so strongly rely upon the statement. So I would suggest to you that to get a statement is all well and good, but you should not make that the corner stone of your case. You should endeavour to support the confession by other circumstantial or direct evidence which will be sufficient to satisfy the court that the suspected person is the guilty one."

Martin warned that "a statement or confession made by an accused person" had to be given "freely and voluntarily" otherwise it might be declared inadmissible in court. He also warned his audience about being too aggressive during interrogations.

"So, even though you are entitled to ask questions for the purpose of eliciting the facts you are not entitled to ask questions for the purpose of breaking a man down, for the purpose of contradicting him, for the purpose of getting him in a frame of mind where he is willing to make the statement in order to be left alone," said Martin.

He also made some observations about dealing with juvenile offenders.

"When you are questioning young persons, there is, of course, a very heavy onus cast upon the police officer, if he introduces a statement by a young person of 16 or 17 years of age. And I would suggest first that you advise the parents, if you wish to question the boy and give them the opportunity of being present or at least coming to the police station with him," said Martin.

In summing up, the defense attorney urged police to avoid developing tunnel vision during investigations.

"I would suggest that perhaps more cases are lost by police officers jumping to a conclusion too quickly than from any other cause," noted Martin.

Certainly this was very true with Ronald Moffatt. The entire case against him largely rested on a confession made under extreme duress. As Moffatt discovered—and the Central Park Five would learn decades later—a confession can trump almost any other piece of courtroom evidence.

Martin's star lawyer, Patrick Hartt noted this tendency himself. In the Archives of the Law Society of Upper Canada, there is a letter Hartt wrote about the power of confessions. The note is dated August 6, 1957 and written on letterhead from Martin's law firm.

"In actual fact, a magistrate, hearing admissions that a confession is true, would in all probability admit the confession. If he did not admit it, it would be virtually impossible for him to obliterate this admitted fact from his mind when attempting to decide on the evidence the guilt or innocence of the accused," wrote Hartt.

Interestingly, Hartt wasn't writing about Ronald Moffatt. His letter concerned an article in a legal journal about the admissibility of confessions. In a broader sense, however, Hartt's words underscore the power of confessions in deciding cases, a fact that remains true even today.

"We love confessions, because it's completely counterintuitive that someone would injure themselves with their own words," says Prof. Young.

Chapter Ten - Ron Today

It is June 24, 2016. I am sitting at a table at the View Restaurant and Bar at a Delta Hotel in Sault Ste. Marie, Ontario. My lunch guests are Ronald Moffatt and his wife, Debbie. My girlfriend Jeanne Enright is also sitting with us. After years of communicating via email, phone and Skype, this is the first time I have met Moffatt face-to-face. He is a handsome older man, with white hair and friendly eyes, wearing light-coloured pants and a blue striped causal shirt. His wife is warm, congenial and very supportive of her husband.

Moffatt had originally contacted me on September 21, 2012. He had discovered the book I wrote about Steven Truscott, and sent me an email, explaining how he had a similar story to tell. I was immediately intrigued, and we shared messages. I confirmed the outline of Moffatt's account of wrongful conviction by checking old newspaper articles from the 1950s. The murder of Wayne Mallette had been front-page news in Toronto in the fall of 1956. The arrest and trial of Ron Moffatt had also been extensively covered. The subsequent murders of Gary Morris and especially Carole Voyce, followed by the arrest and conviction of Peter Woodcock were even bigger news. As Woodcock was tried as an adult, his name was used in newspaper accounts of his arrest and trial. Moffatt was a juvenile, so his name was kept out of the papers.

The Annual Report of the Chief Constable of the City of Toronto for the Year 1956 did however, use Moffatt's full name. As presented to the Board of Commissioners of Police (now called the Toronto Police Services Board), the report cited the arrest, conviction and sentencing of "one Ronald Moffatt, 14 years" in the death of Wayne Mallette.

Moffatt was also named in Mark Bourrie's 1997 book *By Reason of Insanity*, which covered Woodcock's early life and murder spree. For reasons of privacy, Moffatt is identified as "Ronald Mowatt" in the original version of this book (a revised edition includes interviews with Moffatt and spells his last name properly). Bourrie's book was further confirmation that the horrifying story Moffatt was telling me was true (I didn't see the Chief Constable report until much later). Bourrie also cited Moffatt by name in an opinion piece printed in the *Toronto Star* January 17, 2016 entitled, "Why Innocent Kids Confess to Crimes".

Moffatt turns up in the 2004 book *Serial Killers* by Peter Vronsky, which has a chapter about Peter Woodcock. Once again, Moffatt's last name is spelled "Mowatt".

Beyond these references, however, no one had written a complete book about Moffatt's wrongful conviction. There was a very human side to the story as well: unlike

Steven Truscott, Moffatt never received an official apology much less compensation for his arrest and incarceration.

I contacted my publisher, an independent firm called Five Rivers Publishing, and told her about the Moffatt case. We both decided a book was in order. A big problem stood in the way: I had just committed to doing a 120,000 word encyclopedia of infamous American cons and hoaxes for U.S. publisher ABC-CLIO. That project saw me spending all my spare time away from day-to-day journalism researching and writing about Charles Ponzi, Bernie Madoff and Nigerian email scams. The Moffatt project unfortunately had to be put on a backburner for a while.

Moffatt was patient with all the delays. We kept in regular contact and he frequently sent me new information about his case—newspaper articles he had found, observations about the various places he had been held in custody, names of people involved in his case. I regularly sent him new questions, trying to drill down and get as many details as I could about his dreadful experience.

And now, my girlfriend and I were here, in Ron Moffatt's adopted hometown of Sault Ste. Marie, meeting the man and his wife for the first time.

Lunch-time conversation ranged between interview questions and personal remarks. Moffatt had a soft-spoken, genial manner. He spoke freely but was not one for making long comments. We observed how modern-day DNA testing could have cleared Moffatt in Mallette's death, as it has cleared other victims of wrongful conviction. Moffatt and Debbie expressed the theory that police knew he was innocent after Woodcock was picked up, but didn't want to admit fault.

"They had egg on their face," noted Debbie.

I mentioned how the chief suspect in the murders of Wayne Mallette, Gary Morris and Carole Voyce was a boy on a bicycle.

"I couldn't ride a bike," said Moffatt.

"Still can't," added Debbie.

"I had a poor sense of balance. I used to box as a kid. I think my inner ear [got screwed up]. You should see me walk. I don't walk straight. Like I've had too many," continued Moffatt.

"I tried to get him on a bicycle a couple times," said Debbie.

Moffatt noted he couldn't ice skate either. He reminisced about the ride he worked at the CNE, called the Rotor that spun, pinning people to the walls by the force of gravity even after the floor dropped out.

"This girl, Monique, I don't remember her last name, she used to get on a bike and go around [the inside of the ride]. I used to go on the ride at night, hang out with a buddy from Germany."

Moffatt spoke proudly about his children and step-child and how important his family was to him. Moffatt has made a very good life for himself, considering where he came from. He and Debbie enjoy watching Ken Burns documentaries and the Turner Classic Movies network on TV. Moffatt is actively involved in the lives of his children, step-child and grandchildren from both marriages.

During our lunch-time meeting, Moffatt observed again how his parents, highly dysfunctional as they might have been in many other ways, came through for him after his arrest.

"They lost just about everything to pay for the legal part of it," noted Moffatt.

He said his relationship with his parents changed after his acquittal. They weren't close, and they weren't able to discuss what Moffatt had been through.

Moffatt thought about what life would have been like, had he not been arrested and convicted.

"I probably would have went right through school, got a better education. I wouldn't have had all the emotional problems I had. Probably would have end up having a better job," he said.

Moffatt instantly corrected himself, noting he "did have a good job" and enjoyed his time working as a school caretaker. That said, he once had higher ambitions.

"I wanted to be an architect. When I was young, I also thought about commercial art. Everyone said, 'Go into commercial art. Go into commercial art," he said.

While he never became a commercial artist, Moffatt did enjoy doing landscape paintings, water colours and sketches, in addition to his cartooning.

Moffatt has never read Isabel LeBourdais' 1966 book, *The Trial of Steven Truscott*. The book that apparently might have included his own story, had he been able to talk about it at the time. While Moffatt is a prolific reader, of history among other topics, he said LeBourdais' work is too emotionally searing for him to handle.

It took a very long time for Moffatt to come to terms about what happened to him. He kept his experience secret, even from his immediate family.

"I remember one day, Ronnie said 'I have to tell you something' and he told me and it was like, he carried a lot of shame with him his whole life and that's why he didn't want to tell me. He told me, 'Promise not to tell anyone.' I understood when he told me why he was like he was about a lot of things in life. Why he kept things so private. People would ask him about his history in Toronto and he'd always shuffle it off. He'd say, 'I don't remember too much about Toronto'. To me, it was a tragedy," noted Debbie.

In a previous correspondence, Moffatt said he wasn't able to tell his own children what had happened to him until they were into their thirties.

"When I started relating it to them they were already aware of the circumstances. Apparently without my knowledge, both my mother and [first] wife had discussed it with them. They were shocked and horrified about all that I had went through and felt I was owed something from the authorities," Moffatt had written.

When interviewed, Moffatt's daughter, Cathy Anne Moffatt, expresses a deep love for her father and horror at what he went through. Cathy was born in Woodstock, Ontario in 1962.

"My mother believed that her children should not hear negative things about my dad. She gave me tidbits of information as she deemed my level of maturity could handle them. The simple truth, according to her, was that dad had a very hard life and that we should show him empathy and compassion," states Cathy Anne, in response to written questions I sent her.

"I have often pushed dad to talk to me about his 'time' spent in juvenile detention and he always changed the subject, simply because it was too painful. Perhaps his age prompted him, perhaps it's your influence, but he now speaks liberally about it with me. Pardon the vulgarity (dad never permitted that I be vulgar) but it's about fucken time that he stopped feeling guilty for things he could not control ... My dad had every reason to feel broken. Yet he still walked with his head high," she continues.

In other emails, Moffatt outlined some additional thoughts he had about his trial.

Asked what lessons he hoped the public would take away from his ordeal, he wrote: "That police should never be allowed to interrogate underage persons without the presence of either a parent/guardian or legal counsel. I also believe when a juvenile is charged with any serious crime that they should have the right to have their case judged by a jury of their peers just the same as adults have that choice. In my case I felt that during my initial trial the judge had made up his mind early in the trial that I was guilty and seemed to completely ignore all evidence presented by my lawyer that proved otherwise."

We chatted about other Canadians who have been wrongly convicted, such David Milgaard, Guy Paul Morin, Donald Marshall and especially, Steven Truscott.

Moffatt regrets he's never met Truscott. Indeed, they would have much to talk about. As mentioned, there are several eerie parallels between the two boys' cases. There are several significant differences too, however. Moffatt served eight months in custody. After being convicted September 30, 1959, Truscott was originally sentenced to death. This was later commuted to life. Interestingly, Truscott served some of his sentence at the Ontario Training School for Boys at the Guelph Reformatory, albeit years after Moffatt had departed from the place.

Beyond the severity of their sentences, the cases of Moffatt and Truscott diverged in another major way. Because his name was kept out of the papers, Moffatt's name is unknown to most of the public. Truscott by contrast was tried as an adult and named in the media. Truscott's case became so well known it became something of a cause célèbre. LeBourdais' hugely controversial book was debated in the House of Commons (politicians were shocked at the time at the notion of anyone—much less a woman journalist—suggesting police and courts might actually make a mistake) and led to an unprecedented review by the Supreme Court of Canada. As noted previously, G. Arthur Martin helped with Truscott's appeal to the

Supreme Court. In a May 4, 1967 ruling, the Supreme Court upheld Truscott's original verdict. There was still quite a bit of doubt about his conviction, however, and Truscott was paroled in September, 1969.

Truscott's case remained in the news, with subsequent books after his release, while Moffatt's case faded into obscurity. Truscott ended up living in Guelph, working as a factory millwright. He married and had children. Under the law, however, he was still a convicted murderer. In 1997, inspired by the examples of Milgaard and Morin (whose murder convictions were overturned following the introduction of DNA evidence that exonerated them), Truscott contacted AIDWYC to clear his name. Three years later, Truscott appeared on camera in a CBC-TV documentary about his case. The documentary underlined how slipshod the police investigation of Truscott had been (other suspects were largely ignored as authorities zeroed in on Truscott, who was given an intense police interrogation without a parent or lawyer present, just like Moffatt). After the program aired, AIDWYC announced it was going to approach the federal Justice Minister to review Truscott's case.

On November 29, 2001, AIDWYC presented the Minister of Justice with an extensive report, pointing to new evidence and new suspects. Two months later, the federal government announced the Truscott case would be reviewed. After much governmental to-and-fro, the Ontario Court of Appeal launched a three-week review, in June 2006. On August 28, 2007, the Court acquitted Truscott of the murder of Lynne Harper.

"You asked about the other famous cases in which innocent men such as Steven Truscott were imprisoned for crimes they didn't commit. Absolutely deplorable what these men went through and I am elated that they finally received some degree of justice. However, even though they were finally exonerated and awarded compensation, it still doesn't give them back the years they lost from their lives being imprisoned and the shame of being tagged a degenerate and even though you have been cleared there are still those out there who have doubts about you. Saying that, I still believe that I have not received my dues from those who persecuted me," Moffatt wrote, in an email sent prior to our face-to-face meeting.

There remains one final major difference between Moffatt's case and that of Truscott: after his acquittal, then Ontario Attorney General Michael Bryant issued an official apology to Truscott on behalf of the province. On July 7, 2008, Truscott received $6.5 million in compensation from the Ontario government.

Moffatt, by contrast, hasn't received any official recognition of the harm done to him.

"I feel I deserve something from them as it was a horrific experience and it affected my life for years. I am hoping that if you agree to write this story of mine that it may prompt maybe a law firm, an advocate, or even the general public to take up my cause and embarrass the authorities into compensating me ... I only wish my parents were still alive, I would give most of what I received to them as they almost lost everything fighting for my freedom ... If I am ever awarded anything, I will give some of it to my three children and my stepdaughter. I am near the end of my life and though my wife and I are far from rich, we are doing fine," he wrote, in emails.

In the summer of 1957, a few weeks after his acquittal but prior to his ill-fated involvement in the Joker Gang, Moffatt found himself walking along College Street in downtown Toronto, near the police station where he'd been interrogated. It was a stretch of city where he regularly strolled, despite the unpleasant history it held for him. To his surprise, Moffatt spotted Inspector Adolphus Payne exiting a police cruiser in front of the station.

"He recognized me and called me over" recalls Moffatt.

Overcoming his inherent fear of policemen—and Inspector Payne in particular—Moffatt approached.

"He asked how I was doing. I wasn't interested in talking to him and just wanted to get away and yet he kept going on about how sorry he was about what happened, blah, blah. I was cordial but underneath I was very upset that I was being confronted by the S.O.B. who was to blame for my nightmare. Ironically, this is the only apology I ever received from the authorities," states Moffatt.

In the very first message Moffatt ever sent me, he added another observation: "I guess I just feel even though I was finally acquitted, I still don't feel completely satisfied and feel the authorities owe me more than, 'OOPS. WE'RE SORRY!"

Afterword

One frustration when dealing with a decades-old criminal case is that it's impossible to apply modern forensic principles to determine guilt or innocence beyond a shadow of doubt. Today, the presence of viable DNA evidence means authorities can determine with almost 100 percent certainty who did or didn't commit a murder. Consider this: little Wayne Mallette had bite marks on his body. If DNA matching that of Peter Woodcock was found in these marks, then Woodcock was the killer. The same applies for Ron Moffatt. This science, however, was not available to Toronto police back in the 1950s.

Without DNA, Ron Moffatt's fate is similar to that of Steven Truscott's: acquitted but not completely exonerated in the eyes of the law.

Having said that, a careful review of facts does point, with as much certainty as can be had, to Peter Woodcock's guilt and Moffatt's innocence.

But what about Moffatt's confession?

As Chapter Eight notes, false confessions are far more common than people think. And Moffatt's experience with police (juvenile offender with no parent or lawyer present during interrogation, leading questions, threats, etc.) is almost a textbook case about how false confessions are generated. Authorities admitted they had little else to go on besides Moffatt's supposed confession. In a letter to Wayne Mallette's father, Det. Bernard Simmonds cited "a lack of corroboratory evidence and sufficient doubt through medical evidence, etc.," to explain Moffatt's 1957 acquittal.

Woodcock was also interrogated without a parent, guardian or lawyer present. There's plenty of proof, however, to confirm Woodcock was being truthful.

Woodcock was a severely maladjusted boy with a history of molesting and assaulting children. Months before Wayne Mallette was murdered, Woodcock lured a little girl to the Don Valley. When police located the girl, she was huddled with Woodcock inside a phone booth. Woodcock later admitted he had planned to kill the girl with a knife. Woodcock said he molested multiple children around Toronto. Police in turn interviewed several boys and girls who had either been approached or molested by a teenager on a bicycle who matched Woodcock's description.

In Mark Bourrie's book, *By Reason of Insanity*, Woodcock described how he murdered Wayne Mallette (though without offering any contrition for the killing): "I shoved his face down into the dirt, and he stopped breathing. I knew he was gone when I heard the death rattle," stated Woodcock, of his encounter with Wayne at the CNE.

Mallette's murder followed the same pattern as the

subsequent murders of Gary Morris and Carole Voyce. In all three cases, a young child was approached by a teenager on a bicycle, then molested and brutalized before being murdered. While no one saw Woodcock kill these kids, plenty of people noticed him before or after the crimes had been committed. An observant night watchman at the CNE had a weird conversation with a murder-minded teenager with a bicycle the night Mallette was killed. Morris and Voyce were both abducted in front of child witnesses who described a youth on a bike who looked like Peter Woodcock. After killing Voyce, Woodcock was seen by a number of witnesses, including a yardman in the Don Valley who told police about a dark-haired boy pushing a bicycle on some rail tracks.

Moffatt was in custody when Morris and Voyce were killed. Moffatt also says poor balance meant he couldn't ride a bike. His mother said the same thing to reporters at the time of her son's trials.

Woodcock, on the other hand, was very much a cycling enthusiast.

"When I was living at home, especially in my teenage years, I rode my bike everywhere. You can go places on a bicycle that people on foot would need a long time to get into," stated Woodcock to crime writer Bourrie.

Woodcock's bike-riding prowess was verified by authorities at the Sunnyside Children's Centre, the media and his own foster family. A *Toronto Daily Star* story from January, 1957, referred to Woodcock's bicycle as his "prize possession."

Another important fact: Woodcock continued to kill even as an adult. After getting a day-pass following decades of institutionalization, Woodcock promptly murdered fellow patient, Dennis Kerr in 1991, with the help of a duped comrade. Following that episode, Woodcock calmly walked into a police station and informed the startled officers what he had just done. He told them where Kerr's body was then, according to police reports, proceeded to masturbate repeatedly while being held in custody. Police went to where Woodcock directed them and discovered a corpse and a crime scene that matched what he'd told them.

Given such behaviour, there's no reason to doubt the veracity of Woodcock's admissions.

Likewise, the description of the boy seen by the watchman at the CNE grounds on the night of September 15, 1956 (short, dark-haired) matches Woodcock, not Moffatt (who was taller and light-haired).

Several witnesses placed Moffatt at the Metro Theatre at the time of Mallette's killing. And none of these witnesses reported anything amiss about him. If a normal teenager—that is, someone other than Peter Woodcock—had just killed a little kid with their bare hands, you might expect them to be a bit shocked, hysterical or out-of-sorts.

To be fair, it's understandable why police acted so swiftly. They were under tremendous pressure to solve an awful child murder that happened during an era when Toronto experienced less than a dozen homicides a year. Moffatt seemed like a good suspect, being familiar with the CNE, about the same age as the cyclist the night watchman conversed with, and going into hiding after Mallette's murder.

That all said, on a personal note, I wouldn't have written this book if I thought Ron Moffatt was guilty.

If Moffatt's quick arrest suggests sloppy police work, his eventual acquittal can be attributed to clever police work. It was a group of North York police officers, remembering a previous case involving a creepy boy named Peter Woodcock that lead to the eventual unravelling of Moffatt's conviction.

Moffatt's story points to a larger issue: even in the worst murder cases, it pays to be cautious, work slowly and not jump to any conclusions. At least not before DNA firmly establishes if police have the right suspect or if the real killer is still at large, planning more killings as Peter Woodcock did.

Selected Bibliography

Newspapers

"Adjourn Hearing Of Boy's Appeal." *The Globe and Mail*, March 2, 1957.

"Allege Boy, 17, Killer." *Toronto Daily Star*, January 22, 1957.

Barker, Gerald. "North York Police Recall June Case Is Lead To Arrest." *Toronto Daily Star*, January 22, 1957.

Beaufoy, John. "A Law Reformer is Disheartened." *The Globe and Mail*, November 16, 1974.

"Bernard Simmonds Was Deputy Police Chief." *The Toronto Star*, June 29, 1991.

"Board May Probe Threat Report In Juvenile Case." *The Globe and Mail*, May 18, 1957.

"Boy Choked to Death." *The Kingston Whig-Standard*, September 19, 1956.

"Boy Guilty In Choking Reform Program Planned." *Toronto Daily Star*, December 5, 1956.

"Boy Murdered in CNE Grounds Seized While Watching Trains." *Toronto Daily Star*, September 17, 1956.

"Boy on Trial In CNE Death." *The Globe and Mail*, October 24, 1956.

Bovsun, Mara. "Psycho Peter Woodcock Murdered Three Children in Late 1950s, Underwent Cutting-Edge LSD

Therapy at Mental Hospital and Killed Again in 1991 When Given Day of Freedom." *New York Daily News*, November 30, 2013.

Bourrie, Mark. "The Serial Killer They Couldn't Cure Dies Behind Bars." *The Toronto Star*, March 9, 2010.

Bourrie, Mark. "Why Innocent Kids Confess to Crimes." *The Toronto Star*, January 17, 2016.

"Bring Back the Death Penalty. Bring Back Our Police!" Advertisement in various New York City newspapers, May, 1989.

Bryant, George. "Psychology, Logic, Brains, Alertness Finally Courage Resulted in Boyd's Capture." *Toronto Daily Star*, March 17, 1952.

Callwood, June. "National Law Reform Commission Gets New Lease on Life." *The Globe and Mail*, May 28, 1986.

Callwood, June. "The Informal Patrick Hartt." *The Globe and Mail*, November 17, 1975.

"Charge Boy, 14, In CNE Slaying." *The Globe and Mail*, September 25, 1956.

"Charge Manslaughter in CNE Boy's Death." *Toronto Daily Star*, September 24, 1956.

"Check Dozen Other Attacks On Children." *Toronto Daily Star*, January 23, 1957.

"CNE Case Reopened May Free Boy." *The Telegram*, January 23, 1957.

"CNE Watchman May Have Clue In Boy Murder." *Toronto Daily Star*, September 18, 1956.

Claridge, Thomas. "Court Rejects Psychopath's Transfer Bid." *The Globe and Mail*, July 9, 1994.

Clarke, Katrina. "What's Going on at the Metro Theatre?" *The Toronto Star*, March 8, 2015.

"'Clues' Pour In." *Toronto Daily Star*, January 21, 1957.

"Commit Boy, 14, In Mallette Case." *The Globe and Mail*, February 2, 1957.

"Confession Is Not Proof Of Guilt." *Toronto Daily Star*, May 18, 1957.

"Court Adjourns Appeal Motion In CNE Death." *The Globe and Mail*, January 25, 1957.

"Court Finds Delinquency in Boy's Death." *The Globe and Mail*, December 5, 1956.

Creighton, Douglas. "Guard Carol's Pal." *The Telegram*, January 21, 1957.*

"Discover Teeth Marks On Body of Slain Boy, 9." *The Globe and Mail*, October 11, 1956.

"Doctors Tell Court They Think Woodcock Is Criminally Insane." *The Globe and Mail*, April 11, 1957.

Doherty, Brennan. "Sept. 1, 1956: Soviet Delegation Visits the Ex." *The Toronto Star*, September 1, 2017.

Echenberg, Alan. "Williams Case Was Fascinating, Perplexing and Distressing." *Ottawa Jewish Bulletin*, November 8, 2010.

Feeny, Edwin. "Liked His Bicycle Very Much—Boy, 4." *Toronto Daily Star*, January 21, 1957.

"Find Dead Boy at CNE Not Victim of Pervert." *The Globe and Mail*, September 18, 1956.

"For A Fair Trial." *Toronto Daily Star*, October 11, 1958.

"Footsteps In The Snow Left A Trail To Her Murder." *The Telegram*, January 21, 1957.

"Free Boy of 15 in Wayne Mallette Murder at CNE." *Toronto Daily Star*, May 17, 1957.

"'Insane' – Judge." *Toronto Daily Star*, April 11, 1957.

"Judge Commits Boy To School In CNE Death." *Toronto Daily Star*, February 1, 1957.

"Leg Bears Tooth Mark After Boy's Odd Death." *The Globe and Mail*, September 19, 1956.

"Light in the Darkness." *The Globe and Mail*, April 13, 1957

Mallette, Irene. "Mother Had Premonition Wayne Not Coming Back From 'This Sinful City'." *Toronto Daily Star*, September 17, 1956.

Malling, Eric. "Laws Should Be So Simple People Don't Need Lawyers." *The Toronto Star*, March 23, 1972.

Manthorpe, Jonathan. "Infighting Leaves Hartt Report in Shreds." *The Toronto Star*, April 5, 1978.

"Manslaughter In CNE Death Charge On Boy." *The Telegram*, September 24, 1956.

McClement, Fred. "Foster Family Is Stunned Gave Peter Everything." *Toronto Daily Star*, January 22, 1957.

McFadden, Robert and Saulny, Susan. "A Crime Revisited: The Decision; 13 Years Later, Official Reversal in Jogger Attack." *New York Times*, December 6, 2002.

"Murder Is Basis Of Police Probe In Death Of Boy." *The Telegram*, September 18, 1956.

Murray, Colin. "'I've Lost Carol' Lost ... Forever." *The Telegram*, January 21, 1957.

"Mystery of Boy's Death Still Unsolved by Police." *The Kingston Whig-Standard*, September 18, 1956.

"Mystery Seen As Boy Dies In CNE Bush." *The Globe and Mail*, September 17, 1956.

"No Murder Charge to Be Laid Against Boy in CNE Killing." *The Kingston Whig-Standard*, September 24, 1956.

"Not Guilty Plea Entered By Juvenile." *The Kingston Whig-Standard*, September 25, 1956.

O'Neil, Dorothy. "Henry Bull: A Fighter, but No 'Gangbuster'." *Toronto Daily Star*, September 4, 1968.

"Patrick Hartt Named to Join Supreme Court." *The Globe and Mail*, June 23, 1966.

"Pervert Suspected But Lad's Killing May Be Mishap." *The Telegram*, September 17, 1956

"Peter Woodcock, 18, Committed for Trial In Slaying of Girl, 4." *The Globe and Mail*, March 27, 1957.

"Peter Woodcock Will Testify At Boy's Retrial." *The Globe and Mail*, May 4, 1957.

Petlock, Bert. "Boy Confessed Murder For Fame—Freed." *The Telegram*, May 17, 1957.

"Police Find Lad Killed in Scuffle." *The Kingston Whig-Standard*, September 22, 1956.

"Post 24-Hour Guard on Boyd." *Toronto Daily Star*, March 17, 1952.

"Reopen Probe of Boy's Death at Ex." *The Globe and Mail*, January 24, 1957.

"Report Peter Handicapped From Infancy." *Toronto Daily Star*, January 22, 1957.

"Reported Lost, 14-Year Old Held In Death of Boy." *The Globe and Mail*, September 22, 1956.

Ross, Selena. "Romeo Phillion, Wrongfully Convicted for Murder, Dies at 76." *The Globe and Mail*, November 3, 2015.

Rusk, James. "Victorious Moscoe Gains Meeting With the Mayor." *The Globe and Mail*, June 30, 1999.

"Russians Pay Secret Visit to CNE in Three Black Cars." *Toronto Daily Star*, September 1, 1956.

"Sadist Killed Gary Morris, 9, Police Believe." *Toronto Daily Star*, October 11, 1956.

Salaam, Yusef. "'It Feels As If I'm On Trial All Over Again'." *The Toronto Star*, October 13, 2016.

"Seeleys Bay Lad, 7, Said Murder Victim." *The Kingston Whig-Standard*, September 17, 1956.

"Tells Murder Details, Woodcock Statement Is Read in Courtroom." *The Globe and Mail*, April 10, 1957.

"The Case of the Central Park Jogger." *New York Times*, August 19, 1990.

"This Boy Wanted." *Toronto Daily Star*, January 21, 1957.

"This Describe Your Son? Your Duty To Report Him." *The Telegram*, January 21, 1957.

Thomas, Gwyn (Jocko). "Adolphus Payne 'Canada's Greatest Detective' Dies at 72." *The Toronto Star*, July 8, 1981.

Thomas, Gwyn (Jocko). "Confession in CNE Case Slaying Said Untrue, May Free Boy." *Toronto Daily Star*, January 23, 1957.

Thomas, Gwyn (Jocko). "'Greatest Detective' Metro's Payne Retiring." *The Toronto Star*, February 7, 1974.

Thomas, Gwyn (Jocko). "Hold Terror-Stricken Boy, 14, In Death Of Lad At Exhibition." *Toronto Daily Star*, September 22, 1956.

Thomas, Gwyn (Jocko). "Sure Carol's Killer Also Slew Boy, Nine, Reward Now $7,000." *Toronto Daily Star*, January 21, 1957.

"Top Deputy Chief Leaves Police Force in Surprise Move," *The Toronto Star*, January 31, 1976.

"Top Prosecutor in Metro, York Lectured in U.S." *The Globe and Mail*, September 4, 1968.

"$2,000 Reward For Information On Boy's Slayer." *The Globe and Mail*, September 21, 1956.

Tyler, Tracey. "Officials Chose Killer as Escort for Sex Slayer." *The Toronto Star*, August 10, 1991.

Tyler, Tracey. "Panel Grapples With Man's Refusal of Psychiatric Help." *The Toronto Star*, March 11, 2002.

Vynhak, Carola. "'50s Woodcock Murders Outraged Toronto." *The Toronto Star*, September 3, 2017.

Wallace, Kenyon. "School Abuse Whistleblowers Were Ignored by Province." *The Toronto Star*, December 11, 2017.

Wallace, Kenyon. "Secret Settlements." *The Toronto Star*, December, 10, 2017.

Wallace, Kenyon. "Training School Lawsuit Launched." *The Toronto Star*, December 12, 2017.

"Woodcock Not Guilty Because of Insanity, To Be Held in Hospital." *The Globe and Mail*, April 12, 1957.

"Woodcock On Trial, Pleads Not Guilty." *Toronto Daily Star*, April 8, 1957.

"Woodcock to be Chief Witness." *The Globe and Mail*, May 14, 1957.

"Young Father Himself P.C. Found Carol Body." *Toronto Daily Star*, January 21, 1957.*

"Youth Held In Boy's Death." *The Telegram*, September 22, 1956.

"Youth Killed Boy, 7." *The Telegram*, September 19, 1956.

"Youth, 17, Charged In Murder of Carole." *The Globe and Mail*, January 22, 1957.

*Newspapers at the time spelled Carole Voyce's name two different ways: Carol and Carole. The correct spelling, according to records, is Carole Voyce. This is how I spelled her name throughout my book. I used "Carol" in some of the entries in the bibliography to reflect how her name was spelled in certain newspaper headlines at the time.

Books

Batten, Jack. *Learned Friends: A Tribute to Fifty Remarkable Ontario Advocates, 1950 – 2000*. Toronto: Irwin Law, 2005.

Bexon, Sandy and Bill Healey. *Bowmanville Training School Through the Years*. 1988.

Bourrie, Mark. *By Reason of Insanity: The David Michael Krueger Story*. Toronto: Dundurn, 1997.

Bourrie, Mark. *Peter Woodcock: Canada's Youngest Serial Killer*. Toronto: R. J. Parker Publishing, 2016 (updated Kindle e-book version of *By Reason of Insanity*).

Feld, Barry. *Kids, Cops and Confessions: Inside the Interrogation Room*. New York: New York University Press, 2012.

Hendley, Nate. *Edwin Alonzo Boyd: The Life and Crimes of Canada's Master Bank Robber*. Toronto: James Lorimer & Company, 2011.

Hendley, Nate. *Steven Truscott: Decades of Injustice*. Neustadt, Ontario: Five Rivers Publishing, 2012.

Hoshowsky, Robert J. *The Last To Die*. Toronto: Dundurn Press, 2007.

Mann, W.E. *Society Behind Bars: A Sociological Scrutiny of Guelph Reformatory*. Toronto: Social Science Publishers, 1967.

Ronson, Jon. *The Psychopath Test*. New York: Riverhead Books, 2011.

Shorter, Edward editor. *TPH: History and Memory of the Toronto Psychiatric Hospital, 1925 – 1966*. Toronto: Wall & Emerson, Inc. 1996.

Trainum, James L. *How The Police Generate False*

Confessions. Lanham, Maryland: Rowman & Littlefield, 2016.

Vronsky, Peter. *Serial Killers.* New York: The Berkley Publishing Group, 2004.

Websites/Online Articles

Canada's Historic Places. (http://www.historicplaces.ca/)

Innocence Canada, formerly the Association in Defence of the Wrongly Convicted. (https://www.aidwyc.org/)

Harland-Logan, Sarah. "Romeo Phillion." Innocence Canada, formerly the Association in Defence of the Wrongly Convicted. (http://innocencecanada.com/exonerations/romeo-phillion/)

McKenzie, Victoria. "Most States Still Deny Juveniles Access to Counsel: Report." (https://thecrimereport.org/2017/05/18/most-states-still-deny-juveniles-access-to-counsel-50-years-after-gault-ruling-report-finds/), posted May 18, 2017.

Ontario Shores Centre for Mental Health Sciences. (https://www.ontarioshores.ca/)

Ramsland, Katherine. "These Crimes Are Not for Sensitive Ears." (https://www.psychologytoday.com/blog/shadow-boxing/201602/these-crimes-are-not-sensitive-ears), posted February 7, 2016.

Seward, Chris. "Researchers: More Than 2,000 False Convictions in Past 23 Years." (http://www.msnbc.com/msnbc/researchers-more-2000-false-convi), posted May 21, 2012.

The Innocence Project – Osgoode Hall Law School. (http://www.osgoode.yorku.ca/programs/jd-program/clinics-intensives/innocence-project/)

The Law Society of Upper Canada Archives. (http://www.lsuc.on.ca/PDC/Archives/Overview-of-the-Archives/)*

* The Law Society of Upper Canada (LSUC) is now called the Law Society of Ontario. It was known as the Law Society of Upper Canada, however, when I visited the Archives.

Periodicals/Reports/Documents

Annual Report of the Department of Reform Institutions Province of Ontario for the Year Ending 31st March 1957. Printed by Order of the Legislative Assembly of Ontario, 1958.

Annual Report of the Chief Constable of the City of Toronto for the Year 1956. Toronto: The Noble Scott Company, Limited, Printers.

Assorted Toronto and Metropolitan Toronto Police memos, directives and other documents.

Balko, Radley. "Wrongful Convictions: How Many Innocent Americans are Behind Bars?" *Reason*, Vol. 43, No. 3, July, 2011.

Barrett, Sylvia. "Bad Influence." *Saturday Night*, Vol. 111, No. 5, June, 1996.

Bennett, John. *The Educational Programme of the Ontario Training Schools of the Department of Reform Institutions.* Ontario Training Schools Advisory Board, 1959.

Canada Year Book 1957/1958. Ottawa: Dominion Bureau of Statistics, Information Services Division, Canada Year Book Section, 1958.

Canada Year Book 1959. Ottawa: Dominion Bureau of Statistics, Information Services Division, Canada Year Book Section, 1959.

First Annual Report of the Law Reform Commission of Canada 1971/1972. Department of Justice Canada.

Martin, G.A. "The Admissibility of Confessions and Statements." *The Criminal Law Quarterly*, Vol. 5, No. 1, June, 1962.

Macfarlane, John. "The First Day at Guelph." *The Globe Magazine*, February 19, 1966

Metropolitan Toronto Police - First Annual Report. Metropolitan Toronto Police, 1957.

Moore, Timothy E. and C. Lindsay Fitzsimmons. "Justice Imperiled: False Confessions and the Reid Technique." *The Criminal Law Quarterly*, Vol. 57, No. 4, 2011.

National Juvenile Defender Center, Access Denied: A National Snapshot of States' Failure to Protect Children's Right to Counsel. The National Juvenile Defender Center, May 2017.

Report to the President – Forensic Science in Criminal Courts: Ensuring Scientific Validity of Feature-Comparison Methods. Executive Office of the President, President's Council of Advisors of Science and Technology, September, 2016.

Young, Professor Alan. *False Confessions: The Attitude and Approach of Canadian Courts*. December 13, 2016.

Videos

Mind of a Murderer: The Mask of Sanity, British Broadcasting Corporation, 2002.

A Bad Trip, Host Hana Gartner, The National Magazine, Canadian Broadcasting Corporation, aired December 19, 1997.

Interviews

Mark Bourrie

Debbie Moffatt

Cathy Anne Moffatt

Ronald Moffatt

Alan Young, Osgoode Hall Law Professor, Director, The Innocence Project

Letters

Letter from Patrick Hartt, August 6, 1957. Law Society of Upper Canada Archives.

Directories

Toronto City Directory: 1954

Toronto City Directory: 1955

Toronto City Directory: 1956

Toronto City Directory: 1957

Speeches

Remarks by G.A. Martin to Porcupine Police School, February 24, 1954. Law Society of Upper Canada Archives.

Ron Moffatt Reports

METROPOLITAN TORONTO POLICE
TORONTO, ONTARIO, CANADA

NAME MAYNARD, Peter Carl Woodcock NO. 186/57
ALIAS
ADDRESS 115 Ly ton Bldv.
CRIME Murder
AGE 17   HEIGHT 5!6
WEIGHT   BUILD slender
HAIR brn.   EYES brn.wears glasses
COMPLEXION Med. Pockmarked CHE
BORN Toronto   OCCUPATION student
DATE OF PHOTO Jan.22/57
OFFICER Det. Crawford N.Y 21
REMARKS

**Arrest notice for Peter Woodcock, January 1957 (Metropolitan
Toronto Police)**

JUVENILE COURT

IN THE ~~COUNTY COURT~~ OF THE COUNTY OF YORK

His Honour

Judge Stewart

{ ....Tuesday................the....7th..day

of............May...................19.57..

THE ~~KING~~ QUEEN VS.   RONALD MOFFATT

Upon the application of the Crown Attorney for the City of Toronto and the County of York, I do hereby order the.....Superintendent.....of the........REFORMATORY.........

at.........................GUELPH..in the County

of...........................WELLINGTON..in the Province of Ontario,

to forthwith deliver.......RONALD MOFFATT...

a prisoner confined in the said.......................REFORMATORY...........................

to...BERNARD SIMMONDS,...a peace

officer, in and for the.......MUNICIPALITY OF METROPOLITAN POLICE, or his deputy

And I do further order the said peace officer to forthwith convey the said...........................

.......................RONALD MOFFATT...

to the City of Toronto in the County of York and there produce and have him before

a...Judge of the Juvenile Court....within and for the said county, to answer to a

certain ~~indictable~~ offence charged against him, to wit..being a juvenile delinquent
he did kill and slay
and thereafter forthwith to reconvey the said...........RONALD MOFFATT................

....

in sure and safe custody to the....................REFORMATORY...............................

at.............................GUELPH...............................and there redeliver him to the

said.....SUPERINTENDENT......................................, unless this court make further order

to the contrary.

(signature)

Judge

**Court document to release Ron Moffatt from Guelph Reformatory for
second trial, May, 1957 (Juvenile and Family Court of the Municipality
of Metropolitan Toronto)**

ONTARIO

THE ONTARIO REFORMATORY
GUELPH, CANADA

May 10/57

RECEIVED FROM THE SUPERINTENDENT, ONTARIO REFORMATORY,

GUELPH, ONTARIO

THE LIVE BODY   MOFFATT,   Ronald   #OTS 425

COMMITTAL WARRANTS   (1   )

PERSONAL CASH $ NIL

GRATUITY $ NIL
                                ALSO:- NIL

PERSONAL EFFECTS AS FOLLOWS:-
   1-Wrist Watch & Bracelet 'n case.
   1-Identification Bracelet. (Ron)
   1-Silver Ring (R.W.)

ESCORTING OFFICER.
TORONTO CITY POLICE

**Items that Ron Moffatt possessed upon release from the Ontario
Reformatory, Guelph. May, 1957 (the Ontario Reformatory, Guelph)**

ONTARIO

THE ATTORNEY-GENERAL'S LABORATORY
PROVINCE OF ONTARIO
87 COLLEGE ST.
TORONTO 5

PHONES
WA. 5-5401, LOCAL 12
EM. 3-1211, LOCAL 2828

Lab. File No.   920-56-S-HJF-PC   October 22, 1956

Your Ref. No.

LABORATORY REPORT

For: Mr. W.O. Gibson, Q.C., Crown Attorney, City Hall, Toronto

Reference: Wayne Mallett - deceased

Copies to: Sergeant of Detectives B. Simmonds, Toronto City Police, 149 College St.,
Toronto

Submitted by........H.J. Fink, B.A.........   Reviewed by..
Biologist

Purpose:

Continuity: Exhibits received from Dr. H. Ward Smith, on September 17, 1956

Exh. No.	Description	Findings
1.	Fingernail scrapings from left and right hands.	Traces of blood found.
2.	Three envelopes labelled, hair from the jack of Wayne Mallett, hair from trousers of Wayne Mallett and hair from the head of Wayne Mallett.	No comparison of these hairs has as yet been attempted.
3.	Cotton swab from mouth of deceased, contained in a bottle.	No significant findings.
4.	Clothing of Wayne Mallett	No evidence of semen found on any of the clothing.
5.	Blood from Wayne Mallett	Group O

Continuity: Exhibits received from Dr. H. Ward Smith, on September 17, 1956

Exh. No.	Description	Findings
1.	Fingernail scrapings from left and right hands.	Traces of blood found.
2.	Three envelopes labelled, hair from the jack of Wayne Mallett, hair from trousers of Wayne Mallett and hair from the head of Wayne Mallett.	No comparison of these hairs has as yet been attempted.
3.	Cotton swab from mouth of deceased, contained in a bottle.	No significant findings.
4.	Clothing of Wayne Mallett	No evidence of semen found on any of the clothing.
5.	Blood from Wayne Mallett	Group O

Report from the Attorney-General's Laboratory regarding examinaton of the body of Wayne Mallette, October, 1956.

36031

```
D D 73      BOY MISSING        6 DIVS.      SEPT. 15-56

   WAYNE  RICHARD   M A L L E T T E

MISSING FROM 42 EMPRESS CRES. SINCE 7:45 P.M. SEPT. 15/56

7 YRS.  MALE, WHITE, SLENDER BUILD, FAIR COMPLEXION, BLOND HAIR,
BROWN EYES, SCAR ON LEFT WRIST,

NEATLY DRESSED, WEARING A BLUE BLAZER   BLUE NYLON SHIRT, BROWN
SHOES.

AUTH:- SGT. O'NEILL  P C ELLERSON            TEAL 10:00 P.M.
```

36032

```
D D 6   REPEATING BOY MISSING   6 DIVS   SEPT. 16-56

REPEATING OF  D D 73 SEPT. 15-56

   WAYNE   RICHARD   M A L L E T T E

MISSING FROM 42 EMPRESS CRES. SINCE 7:45 P M SEPT. 15/56

7 YRS.  MALE, WHITE, SLENDER BUILD, FAIR COMPLEXION, BLOND HAIR,
BROWN EYES, SCAR ON LEFT WRIST

NEATLY DRESSED, WEARING A BLUE BLAZER, BLUE NYLON SHIRT, BROWN
SHOES.

AUTH:- SGT. O'NEILL  P C ELLERSON          FRIEDLANDER..
```

36033

```
 D D 20      BOY LOCATED        6 DIVS      SEPT. 16-56

   WAYNE   RICHARD   M A L L E T T E

MISSING FROM 42 EMPRESS CRES. SINCE 7:45 P M SEPT. 15/56

7 YRS.  MALE, WHITE, SLENDER BUILD, FAIR COMPLEXION, BLOND HAIR,
BROWN EYES, SCAR ON LEFT WRIST

NEATLY DRESSED, WEARING A BLUE BLAZER, BLUE NYLON SHIRT, BROWN
SHOES.

AUTH:- SGT. O'NEILL  P C ELLERSON          FRIEDLANDER..
```

36033

```
D D 20      BOY LOCATED        6 DIVS     SEPT. 16-56

   WAYNE   RICHARD   M A L L E T T E

LOCATED, CANCEL D D 73 SEPT. 15/56 AND D D 6 SEPT. 16/56

AUTH:- SGT. MCDONALD  P C KLUE            FRIEDLANDER 4:28 A.M.
```

Toronto City Police police teletype messages regarding Wayne
Mallette's disapperance. September, 1956 (Toronto City Police).

36035

D D 26 INFORMATION REQUESTED- YOUTH WANTED-DET. DIVS- SEPT. 16-56
        RE BODY OF BOY FOUND DEAD.

ATTENTION ALL STATION SERGEANTS.

                        RE BODY OF BOY FOUND, (WAYNE RICHARD
M A L L E T T E) IN THE EXHIBITION GROUNDS.

ANY INFORMATION FORTHCOMING KINDLY CONTACTT THE SERGEANT OF
DETECTIVES.

THE FOLLOWING IS A DESCRIPTION OF A YOUTH WANTED FOR INVESTIGATION
RE THE ABOVE, WHO WAS SEEN RIDING A BICYCLE ABOUT THIS TIME.

15 YRS. 5'6" 115 LBS. SMALL FACE, THIN BUILD, WEARING A DARK
WINDBREAKER, DARK PANTS, NO HAT. RIDING A DARK BLUE OR BLACK
BICYCLE.

AUTH:- J. NIMMO   ASSISTANT CHIEF OF DETECTIVES O'BRIEN 10:39 A.M.

36036

D D 37 YOUTH WANTED- INVESTIGATION- RE BOY FOUND DEAD- 6 DIV. SEPT.16

Moffatt - Toronto City Police teletype messages regarding the suspect in Wayne Mallette's murder, September, 1956 (Toronto City Police)

INFORMATION WANTED

REWARD

I am authorized to offer a **Reward** of **TWO THOUSAND DOLLARS ($2,000.00)**, to be paid for information leading to the arrest and conviction of the person or persons responsible for the death of **WAYNE MALLETTE**, who died as a result of asphyxiation resulting from the application of manual pressure to the throat, on the evening of Saturday, September 15th, 1956, one hundred yards west of the Dufferin entrance to the Canadian National Exhibition Grounds, and thirty feet south of the fence which is the northern boundary of the said grounds.

WAYNE MALLETTE, seven years of age, was last seen alive at about 7.15 p.m., Saturday, September 15th, 1956, by his brother, apparently heading toward the Dufferin Street entrance to the C. N. E. grounds, alone, he having been playing in the grounds, near the Roller Coaster, during the afternoon.

He was reported missing by his parents, who were visiting this City from Seeley's Bay, Ontario, when he did not return home, and a concerted effort to locate him was initiated. At 2.15 a.m., Sunday, September 16th, the body of **WAYNE MALLETTE** was located by the Police, in a wooded portion of the Canadian National Exhibition grounds referred to above. The deceased youth was lying on his back, but it was evident from dirt on his clothing and face that he had previously been lying face down. Pathological examination revealed that death had resulted from asphyxiation by manual pressure to the throat. A pronounced bite mark, made by human teeth, was evident on the right calf, and a faint marking of a similar nature was on the left buttock.

It has been ascertained that a youth, whose description is given hereunder, approached a Park watchman at about 8.30 p.m., September 15th, 1956, who, in his conversation, indicated he had knowledge that some person had met foul play in the area where **WAYNE MALLETTE**'s body was later located. It is believed this youth is interested in flying and is connected with a youth organization, possibly the Air Cadets, and resides, or has resided, in the north-western portion of the Metropolitan Toronto area, possibly in Weston.

DESCRIPTION: 14-16 years, 5 feet or over, slight build, hair thought to be dark, parted and combed to one side, hair straight--not crew cut, thin face. Was wearing dark windbreaker and dark pants. Spoke rather rapidly, with good diction, in a somewhat boyish voice. Riding a dark coloured bicycle which appeared to be full size, not thought to be a racing type.

I HOLD A WARRANT FOR THE ARREST OF A PERSON OR PERSONS UNKNOWN ON A CHARGE OF MURDER OF WAYNE MALLETTE.

The co-operation and assistance of all citizens and Police Officers is earnestly requested in bringing about the early arrest of the person or persons responsible for the death of WAYNE MALLETTE. The identity of any person supplying information will be treated as confidential, and should there be more than one claimant for the said reward, which is payable in Canadian funds, and expires September 20th, 1957, it shall be apportioned as the Chief of Police of Toronto deems just.

TORONTO CITY POLICE,
149 COLLEGE STREET,
TORONTO 2B, ONTARIO.
Telephone: EM. 2-1711.
September 20th, 1956.

A. E. LEE,
Acting Chief of Police.

Wanted poster for information on Wayne Mallette's killer, September, 1956 (Toronto City Police)

15139

TORONTO CITY POLICE

MISSING PERSON REPORT

OCCURRENCE no

Heron
DETECTIVE ASSIGNED

	DIVISION	DISTRICT
NAME Ronald Moffatt ADDRESS 39 Vanauley Apt. 2	3	

FORMER ADDRESS

PROBABLE DESTINATION   unknown

DATE AND TIME LAST SEEN 7.00 A.M. Sept. 18/56   BY WHOM LAST SEEN Father

CAUSE OF ABSENCE Family indifference   MARITAL STATUS   all

EMPLOYED BY   ADDRESS   TELEPHONE

ATTENDS   Ryerson   HAS RUN AWAY BEFORE   no
         NAME OF SCHOOL

FATHER   Omer Moffatt   ADDRESS 39 Vanauley Apt. 2   TELEPHONE UE.1 1772

MOTHER   Betty "   ADDRESS   "   TELEPHONE

REPORTED BY   mother   ADDRESS   TELEPHONE

RELATIONSHIP   "

FURTHER DETAILS (ALSO GIVE NAMES AND ADDRESSES OF FRIENDS OR RELATIVES, ETC.) Left at 7.00 A.M. Sept. 18/56 with bed a]

clothing & food.

DATE AND TIME LEFT HOME 7.00 A.M. Sept.18/56

LAST SEEN AT 39 Vanauley St.

REPORT RECEIVED BY	RANK	BADGE	THIS REPORT CHECKED BY DIVISION SERGEANT
McInnis	P.C.	472	A/Sgt. Hatton
TELETYPE MSG. NO.	CANCELLED	BULLETIN NO.	CANCELLED	CIRCULAR NO.	CANCELLED
D.D. Feb' 64					

PHYSICAL DESCRIPTION ON OTHER SIDE

Ron Moffatt Missing Persons Report

A Gallery of Ron Moffatt

Dolly Marie (second from left) + Ron Moffatt (second from right)
wedding photo 1961

Debbie Speers and Ron Moffatt

Moffatt 2016

Ron Moffatt retiring

Debbie Speers + her daughter Natasha

Debbie Speers as young woman

Ron Moffatt with pet Buttons

Family Photos

Ron Moffatt and Dolly Marie -1961 wedding

Mother (Bette Moffatt)

Ron Moffatt in 1980

Natasha Cole (Ron Moffatt's stepdaughter) and Paige Cole (Natasha's daughter, Ron's step-daughter)

Natasha Cole (Ron Moffatt's stepdaughter) and Paige Cole (Natasha's daughter, Ron's step-daughter)

Cathy Anne Moffatt, Ron Moffatt's daughter.

Three Generations.

Peter Woodcock booking shot

Metro Theatre 2018 (Nate Hendley in front)

Metro Theatre in 2018 (now an indoor climbing gym)

Ron Moffatt Artwork

About the Author

Nate Hendley is a Toronto-based author who has written several true-crime books. He lives next door to Jeanne Enright, world's greatest girlfriend. Nate wishes to thank Lorina Stephens of Five Rivers Publishing for her interest in this book and infinite patience as I put it together. For more information on Nate's books and background, please visit his website at www.natehendley.com or his blog at https://crimestory.wordpress.com/.

Books by Five Rivers
NON-FICTION

Big Buttes Book: Annotated Dyets Dry Dinner, (1599), by Henry Buttes, with Elizabethan Recipes, by Michelle Enzinas

Al Capone: Chicago's King of Crime, by Nate Hendley

Crystal Death: North America's Most Dangerous Drug, by Nate Hendley

Dutch Schultz: Brazen Beer Baron of New York, by Nate Hendley

The Boy on the Bicycle: A Forgotten Case of Wrongful Conviction in Toronto, by Nate Hendley

John Lennon: Music, Myth and Madness, by Nate Hendley

Motivate to Create: a guide for writers, by Nate Hendley

Steven Truscott, Decades of Injustice by Nate Hendley

King Kwong: Larry Kwong, the China Clipper Who Broke the NHL Colour Barrier, by Paula Johanson

Shakespeare for Slackers: by Aaron Kite, et al
  Romeo and Juliet
  Hamlet
  Macbeth

The Organic Home Gardener, by Patrick Lima and John Scanlan

Shakespeare for Readers' Theatre: Hamlet, Romeo & Juliet, Midsummer Night's Dream, by John Poulson

Shakespeare for Reader's Theatre, Book 2: Shakespeare's Greatest Villains, The Merry Wives of Windsor; Othello, the Moor of Venice; Richard III; King Lear, by John Poulsen

Beyond Media Literacy: New Paradigms in Media Education, by Colin Scheyen

Stonehouse Cooks, by Lorina Stephens

FICTION

Black Wine, by Candas Jane Dorsey

Eocene Station, by Dave Duncan

Immunity to Strange Tales, by Susan J. Forest

The Legend of Sarah, by Leslie Gadallah

The Empire of Kaz, by Leslie Gadallah
  Cat's Pawn
  Cat's Gambit

Growing Up Bronx, by H.A. Hargreaves

North by 2000+, a collection of short, speculative fiction, by H.A. Hargreaves

A Subtle Thing, by Alicia Hendley

The Tattooed Witch Trilogy, by Susan MacGregor
  The Tattooed Witch
  The Tattooed Seer
  The Tattooed Queen

A Time and a Place, by Joe Mahoney

The Rune Blades of Celi, by Ann Marston
  Kingmaker's Sword, Book 1

Western King, Book 2
Broken Blade, Book 3
Cloudbearer's Shadow, Book 4
King of Shadows, Book 5
Sword and Shadow, Book 6
A Still and Bitter Grave, by Ann Marston
Indigo Time, by Sally McBride
Wasps at the Speed of Sound, by Derryl Murphy
A Quiet Place, by J.W. Schnarr
Things Falling Apart, by J.W. Schnarr
A Poisoned Prayer, by Michael Skeet
And the Angels Sang: a collection of short speculative fiction, by Lorina Stephens
Caliban, by Lorina Stephens
From Mountains of Ice, by Lorina Stephens
Memories, Mother and a Christmas Addiction, by Lorina Stephens
Shadow Song, by Lorina Stephens
The Mermaid's Tale, by D. G. Valdron

YA FICTION

Eye of Strife, by Dave Duncan
Ivor of Glenbroch, by Dave Duncan
  The Runner and the Wizard
  The Runner and the Saint
  The Runner and the Kelpie
Avians, by Timothy Gwyn
Type, by Alicia Hendley
Type 2, by Alicia Hendley
Tower in the Crooked Wood, by Paula Johanson
A Touch of Poison, by Aaron Kite
The Great Sky, by D.G. Laderoute
Out of Time, by D.G. Laderoute
Diamonds in Black Sand, by Ann Marston
Hawk, by Marie Powell

WWW.FIVERIVERSPUBLISHING.COM

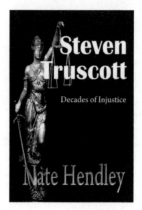

Steven Truscott: Decades of Injustice

ISBN 9781927400210
eISBN 9781927400277
by Nate Hendley
Trade Paperback 6 x 9
November 1, 2012

Imagine being a 14 year-old boy who takes a classmate on a bike ride one spring evening.

In the days to follow, the classmate is found dead and you stand accused of rape and murder. There's no direct physical evidence tying you to the crime, but that doesn't matter. In a lightning fast trial you are convicted and sentenced to death. As far as the press and public are concerned, you are guilty and deserve to die. Such was the fate of Steven Truscott, living with his family on an army base in small-town Ontario in 1959. Read the shocking true story of a terrible case of injustice and the decades long fight to clear Truscott's name.

Very to the point. Fine telling of a local tale ... justice gone wrong. Much praise for Nate Hendley. Very informative.
Goodreads

...It was a great book. It was a page-turner which tells of a boy who none of us ever thought would be at the center of Canadian legal history, all because he was the last person to see his classmate disappear (and die), all because he gave her a bike ride across the bridge towards the highway (where he dropped her off) and saw a car come up.
LibraryThing

Crystal Death

ISBN 9780973927832
eISBN 9780986642340
by Nate Hendley
Trade Paperback 6 x 9
June 1, 2011

A hard-hitting look at the most dangerous illegal drug in North America.

A fact-based account featuring up to the minute interviews and life stories from users, dealers and doctors, with a Canadian perspective on the problem and its potential solutions. An important book for teachers, parents and anyone interested in, or living close to, this devastating drug.

Includes advice on how to talk effectively to your children and students about methamphetamine—and how not to!

This should be in schools, in rehabs, and available to teens and parents. It is not subtle and nor should it be. This is a horrible disease and crisis in our world today and something needs to be done. I hope this book helps. Wonderful work, Mr. Hendley! I pray it reaches the right ears.

Goodreads

I would highly recommend this book for anyone wanting to learn more about this drug.

LibaryThing

CPSIA information can be obtained
at www.ICGtesting.com
Printed in the USA
LVHW081330271119
638722LV00011B/173/P

9 781988 274515